MOLEST

A Guide to Understanding the Impact

of

Physical & Emotional Abuse

DR. LATASHA NESBITT

DR. NES INTERNATIONAL CONSULTING & PUBLISHING

LOS ANGELES COUNTY, CALIFORNIA

Dedication

To all who have endured the trauma
of molestation, it wasn't your fault.
And true freedom can be yours.

To the memory of LaVena Lynn
Johnson whose brutal rape and
murder while serving our country,
still haunts her family and all who
care about injustice.

Dr. Nes International Consulting & Publishing
P.O. Box 70167
Pasadena, CA 91117
www.drnesintl.com

Editor: Stefanie Manns
Cover Design: Octavius Holmes

ISBN: 978-1-949461-14-5

Contents

Introduction

The truth is, I never ever wanted to write this book. It was something I had hoped to avoid, really, for the rest of my life. But no matter how hard I ran away from it; it became evident that God did not agree. In many ways, it was something I felt compelled to make happen. All along, I knew it would be one of the hardest things that I'd ever have to do. I was right. It had become clear regarding what it would mean to abandon a God-given assignment. I surrendered.

I am a book developer; I aid others, mostly first-time authors, complete their own writing projects. There is a great sense of fulfillment that embodies me when I witness their concepts turn into a manifested work. Helping them face their fears and allow others into some of the darkest, saddest times of their lives, even after they have come through it victoriously, is part of what I enjoy doing the most. Telling hard stories is never easy, but in the grand scheme of things, walking them through their process is relatively easy for me. I'm a natural encourager. And while the process can sometimes get grimy, the end result yields a feeling of complete elation, for the both of us. The reward for me is that the world is better as a result of someone being brave enough to tell their truth. Too, the client always experiences another level of spiritual and personal freedom. I was full of all of this encouragement and elation until it was time to take this journey myself. I did once when I penned my neophyte project, *Unfinished Business* in 2015, but this project was different. It was a bit more intimate.

My resistance to this project was two-fold. Firstly, the topic of molestation has essentially become a phenomenon. When I first began research for the project, it seems that high-profile stories, scandals, court cases, and arrests involving sexual assaults and abuse were everywhere. There were documentaries, news stories, and popular talk and reality shows devoted to women and men who were coming forward to share their stories and tell their truths. It seems, to some, that the media has sensationalized the topic, running to print and release every story possible. Not for the purpose of healing, but, more often, for shock and exploitation. The overwhelming headlines have started to create questions. Are the stories real? Are the victims lying? Is this just for ratings? Are people looking to "cash in" on the shocking storyline of trauma, hurt, and pain? Is there anything left to say that has not been said? I didn't want to be accused of sharing my story to become a part of the bandwagon. I've always hated going along with the crowd. This was no different.

But more than that, it was the fear. The second—and the scariest—reason that I was hesitant to write this book was that I didn't want to accept what others had done, actually hurt me. I didn't want to accept that I'd been wounded as deeply as I had, and, that over thirty years later, those memories and experiences could come back to me like they'd just happened yesterday. I didn't want to be judged, or to have anyone think that I was still suffering and therefore 'weakened' but acts done against me. Like all abuse and painful parts of our pasts, I'd decided long ago to put what happened to me away—and keep it there. I knew that writing this book meant that I would have to relive it all. The pain. The shame. The guilt. The confusion. I'd worked so hard to bury those experiences, those parts of myself that had been so hurt and damaged that they were easier to forget than to face.

However, as I approached my fortieth birthday, I knew I had some more unfinished business that needed tending to. I wanted to finally free myself of the excuses I used to not pen this work. Since I know God guided me to write this, it's no surprise that my fortieth year on Earth would be the year to release this project, finally. When we look at Moses in the Bible, 40 is such a significant aspect of his life. Moses lived for 120 years. The first 40 years he spent in the palace, the next 40 years he spent on the back side of the desert, and the last 40 years he devoted to becoming a true servant of God. I used the first 40 years of my life to pursue things I wanted to do. But as I embarked on the second 40 years of my life, I have moved out of the way in hopes of fulfilling assignments that are not only uncomfortable and stretch my own capacity, but that impact the greater good in a way I haven't done before. Being obedient to God at this time of my life, to serve, to free myself and others who are suffering in bondage of trauma and pain is why you are reading these words now. In sharing parts of my story, I want to set us all free.

This is unique in a way. Not only will I share my own story, but I'll explore and examine historical and current accounts of molestation from others, some you may have heard of and some you may not. In these pages you will find data and statistics surrounding sexual abuse, particularly among children, and evidence of how their experiences have impacted their lives. I didn't want to do a full review of the literature regarding Childhood Sexual Abuse (CSA) (there are already a plethora of them out there)[1], but I did want readers to understand the impact and effects of molestation and the widespread trauma that so many victims are silently suffering through.

---

[1] Here is a quick look at some scholarly books and articles on Childhood Sexual Abuse : https://www.questia.com/library/criminal-justice/criminology-and-crime/child-sexual-abuse

The devastation of molestation crosses every line imaginable—race, gender, and class. But the victims whose stories are shared here are all bound by a single truth. Their trust was violated by someone they trusted, and their lives were never same again.

This book brings to light the fact that childhood sexual abuse is one of the most prevalent crimes in society across the globe, but it is one that is talked about the least. It is a crime that no one wants to accept or see. It's common for molestation to be hidden, to remain a secret. The crime and the pain endured as a result are kept in the dark.

As a part of my own healing journey, I researched this topic, and consciously and unconsciously surveyed those around me who have also experienced childhood sexual abuse in an effort to learn as much as I could about its effects and how they'd shown up in my own life. I wanted to share some of what I discovered in this book, including the stories of those who have been molested too, not only to remind anyone who has suffered abuse at the hands of someone they loved and trusted that they are not alone, but also to prove how common these experiences are among the general public. Molestation has been happening behind closed doors for decades, and it's become such a widespread part of our culture, that cycles of childhood sexual abuse have continued practically since the beginning of time. Both the perpetrators and victims are damaged as these cycles continue.

And then there is what I consider to be the most important part of this book, which is the answer to the question, "What do we do about this?" How do we heal? How do we deal with the pain that has destroyed our self-esteem, our sexuality, and rips through our relationships? How do we unpack these experiences so we can trust and love again?

How do we share our stories? How do we protect our children? These are all questions that need answers. While I am not a clinician,[2] I want to explore and prayerfully encourage dialogue through some of what I have written in these pages.

This book is divided into three main sections:

❖ **The Problem:** An in-depth look at the prevalence of childhood sexual abuse and true stories of victims who have suffered in silence.

❖ **The Impact:** A candid look at seven ways your life or the lives of those you love can be impacted by childhood sexual abuse.

❖ **The Strategy:** Practical strategies for healing past pain and growing through the residue of the experiences.

---

[2] At the time this book is written and released, I am not a licensed or clinically trained psychologist or practitioner. I, however, share from an experiential and spiritual revelatory level. My Ph.D. studies focus on the issue of race in American society and the history of American education. ☺

Whether you've been sexually abused or molested by someone you respected, or you love someone who has, I want you to find hope and help here. I want you to find and reclaim a piece of your peace, your identity, and your personal power. Molestation should never, ever, be a best-kept secret. So, this book is for the men and women who never told. Those who felt powerless and unprotected. Those who still, after all these years, feel shattered and broken.

Let's find the healing we all need. When we heal, we can become free. We can become whole.

Section One

THE PROBLEM

The Prevalence of Molestation

The first step to heal childhood trauma is acknowledge that it happened. ~Dr. Thema Bryant[3]

Though an incredibly hard topic for many of us to discuss, molestation is an issue that has impacted millions of people worldwide. Like most crimes, it does not discriminate. People of every gender, race, ethnicity, religion, political affiliation, socioeconomic status, or any other divider for that matter, have suffered at the hands of abusers—often in silence. That silence keeps the victim afraid, ashamed, and also protects the perpetrators, enabling them to continue to abuse again and again. However, in order to help heal a generation, it is necessary for us to shed light on this topic and to tell the truth. It's time for us to talk about the devastation and pain that, for too long, we've kept

---

[3] *Healing from Childhood Trauma*, The Homecoming Podcast with Dr. Thema.

silent to keep everyone around us comfortable and to protect our families, our images, our reputations, and the people we love and respected.

Molestation and rape of children are not new phenomenon.

Unfortunately, for decades, many have suffered silently from the negative effects of molestation and other sexual abuse, left to judge themselves, sit in shame, feeling completely alone. Our silence dates back to the biblical days. Tamar, the daughter of King David, was raped by her half-brother, Amnon. The Bible gives this account of experience:

> But when she brought them near him to eat, he took hold of her, and said to her, 'Come, lie with me, my sister.' She answered him, 'No, my brother, do not force me; for such a thing is not done in Israel; do not do anything so vile!...But he would not listen to her; and being stronger than she was, he forced her and lay with her... (2 Samuel 13:11)

When she revealed what happened to her, Tamar was silenced and relegated to the peripheries of society. Never permitted to marry and therefore childless,

Tamar carried the weight of the sexual abuse with her for years:

> *Her brother Absalom said to her, 'Has Amnon your brother been with you? Be quiet for now, my sister; he is your brother; do not take this to heart.' So Tamar remained, a desolate woman, in her brother Absalom's house.* – 2 Samuel 13:11-12, 14, 20

It is said, that no one defended Tamar until two years later when her brother Absalom avenged her crime by retaliating on her behalf.[4]

The truth is that when sexual abuse involves vulnerable people, despite the horrific experience and the devastation it causes, it is often swept under the rug. When it happens at the hands of people we're related to, there will be family members who will not even consider the acts as crimes. But as renowned therapist Dr. Thema Bryant reminds us, if the action happened prior to the age of 18, the sexual action was indeed a crime.

---

[4] 2 Samuel 13:30 shows how Absalom's men killed Amnon when he was drunk.

Understanding the serious legal, emotional, and spiritual violation that molestation really is, forces us to face the hard facts. Abuse is abuse. A crime is a crime. Molestation of a minor is a crime. Sexually violating someone beyond their consent is criminal no matter their age.

We cannot deny that.

According to *Dictionary.com,* to 'molest' means "to bother, interfere with, or annoy or to make indecent sexual advances to[ward]." "Indecent," by definition, means "to offend against generally accepted standards; improper; vulgar." When we take those words in, let them sit, we can see molestation for what it is. We can cast aside the common, more comfortable descriptions, like "just touching" that society has adopted in attempt to make molestation or rape, an easier pill to swallow, and to ensure that abusers are seen as people instead of the predators they are, all while undermining the victims who are deeply harmed by what's been done to them.

Before we can face the hard truths, I believe it is necessary to, first, define molestation for what it is. Sexual intercourse is molestation. Oral sex is molestation. Touching a child in a sexual way is molestation. And so is exposing a child to pornography or making sexual comments to them. Any and all of these acts are criminal offenses. As a society, we cannot continue to undermine, minimize, and categorize childhood sexual trauma into minor and major offenses. The type of abuse, the age of the abuser or the victim, the circumstances, do not matter. A crime is a crime. All acts of sexual abuse should be treated that way. Molestation is that elephant in the room, that cannot, and should not, be ignored. Keeping the crime in the dark is killing the esteem, spirits, and identities of our children, and only breeding more predators.

The word "molestation" has such a harsh connotation that victims tend to shy away from identifying as someone who has been hurt in that way. We hear attempts to downplay what happened to them, using phrases such as, "touched inappropriately" instead. Maybe you were inappropriately touched, but molested? No, never! That happened to my friend or maybe even her friend or the girl or boy on the news last week in a country far from mine, but never to me! Nope, not me! This is all denial resulting from the shame that victims feel, because as a society, we wrongly persecute the victim instead of the perpetrator. It's pretty embarrassing to understand this truth for what it is—victim blaming.

But when we accept the true meaning of molestation for what it is, we not only acknowledge the pain of the victim, but implicate the abusers.
We can drive the need to have necessary, open conversations about this issue and the harm that

sexual abuse has caused to families and communities all over the world. And we can better understand the complexity of this type of abuse, and its often, long-term effects.

The Impact of Abuse on My Life

While it may not be the case for every person who has been abused sexually, for most, the effects can be damaging. The emotional and spiritual impact of sexual abuse, specifically molestation, can be life altering. When it comes to the impact of molestation on the lives of children, I wrote most of this book not from a quantitative or even a clinical perspective, but from personal experiences and observations. My sexual abuse completely changed my life.

Like other children who are abused, those violations stole my innocence. As a child, I had no way to process and understand my feelings, and I certainly couldn't predict how the abuse would become such a part of me and my identity, so much so that I could not separate who I was from what had happened to me. Through consisting healing with confronting the truth of my pain, I know now, as a 40-year-old woman, that there are certain characteristics, beliefs, and behaviors that have stemmed from significant experiences in my life, including my abuse.

I was born a woman of color, and that shaped me. My father though loving and caring, didn't live inside my home, and that shaped me. I was a victim of police brutality while attending graduate school, that shaped me. I was molested as a little girl and as a young woman, and that undeniably shaped me. It changed me. There was a piece of me that was taken, and I can never get it back.

These experiences stained parts of my childhood and left me feeling confused. I have come to the conclusion that because of early childhood sexual experiences, certain behaviors, most detrimental, have leeched onto the fullness of who I am. And while I've learned to try, as much as I can, to separate my identity from my trauma, what happened to me is a part of my life and who I am. I've had to learn how to deal with that, to accept it, and to work to heal through honesty and the grace of God.

Over the course of my life, I was molested at least three times.

When I was about five years old…

My grandpa was gone that day. This was rare that he'd leave us at home while he went out. My younger sister and I were his side kicks. We accompanied him everywhere he needed to go. You didn't see one of us, without seeing the others. This day was different though, somehow. I don't remember much about why we were left alone at home, with "him." The details are buried in recesses of my mind but come back in pieces.

I do know it wasn't evening time. It was either morning or afternoon. We were in our dining room, and it didn't have a door. The space was accessible in three ways, from three different directions. We could enter the room from my eldest sister's room which was adjacent, from the hallway that led from the bathroom, my mother's bedroom, and from the kitchen.

There were full wooden bunk beds in the room. My Grandpa typically slept there. Sometimes I slept on the top bunk when I wanted to be closer to him. It was a typical bunk bed; a top bed and a bottom bunk which was held together by a ladder on one end. The teenaged boy told me to climb in the bottom bunk bed and move towards the ladder near the edge of the bed. With my bottom on the bottom bed, my feet, hand, and head dangled in between the steps of the ladder. How he wanted me positioned was pretty awkward for my short frame. My bottom sat on one step, and he situated my face in between the one of the ladder's steps so that my chin could rest on it. Shortly after I got situated, he loosened his pants and proceeded to put his penis between the steps on the ladder where my head laid. He placed his penis in my mouth. I wasn't sure what was happening but could tell that he enjoyed the experience. He seemed to have it perfectly planned out. He moved fast, likely anxious that he'd be caught.

Right after the bunk bed fiasco, he rushed me into the bathroom which was only a few steps of where the bunks were. I went inside and sat as a spectator as he thrust his hands back and forth on his penis and semen shot nearly everywhere. I guess he wanted me to witness his excitement following oral sex with a five-year-old.

I don't remember much about that day, but I knew what happened was wrong, and it was something we could both get in trouble for. I also don't remember much of the conversation that day following the incident, but I recall a bit of commotion in the house later that evening as my mom and Grandpa made it home. The tension lasted for a while. I'd told one of my brothers what happened, and I remember him confronting the perpetrator. That may have been what ended the whole ordeal. It never happened again.

When I was about twelve years old…

I was in middle school. I was staying at my Auntie's, and I was napping in one of her bedrooms, in a fetal style position, with my knees almost to my chest. I woke up to one of my cousins attempting to penetrate me. I repositioned my body and the madness stopped. He left the room. I pretended to remain sleep as I listened to him talking with someone outside of the door. I understood fully what happening, but I was flabbergasted at the fact that someone in my own family would commit such an act. I never said anything about it.

When I was about nineteen years old…

It was my sophomore year of college.

In the foggy distance of my nap, I could hear some of the high school girls that I was mentoring laughing and joking and playing music as we rode the bus to tour colleges in a few southern states that year. I was excited about the fact that I, along with a few other members of the organization that I was a part of, was able to provide the experience of exposing girls to the option of a college education. Though we had a long road ahead of us, I was elated to know the girls were embracing their time away from home and enjoying one another. I'd been looking forward to this trip for months, and now we were here.

My nap was interrupted by someone fondling my vagina. I had a few people around me, but I woke from my light nap startled.

The person next to me was also the person who planned the trip. She was the great community organizer. She was the prolific speaker. She was the race-conscious sociologist. She was the quintessential mentor. She was a Christian woman who heralded the message of God adamantly to all that were in her presence and throughout the globe. She embodied the epitome of boldness, the essence of charisma. I looked up to her. I admired her. But what she did that day left me confused. *How could you?*, I thought.

I sat up and looked over at her. She laid next to me but appeared to be napping. I waited for her to get up and acknowledge what she had done and the pain she has inflicted, but there was none. She pretended to be asleep and never bothered to look my way.

I waited it out. I wanted to say something to someone, but I knew the trip wasn't about me. We had 30 plus lives to look after on the trip, and I never wanted that day to be about me. We needed to be sure that each girl got what she needed, that anxieties were in check, that medicines were taken, and every last one of them made it back home safely. They were the priority on that trip. This could wait.

We got to our destination, but my 19-year-old mind needed peace. However, the peace I sought wouldn't come from her. I started to try to justify why she would do something like this to "me..." I remembered that I'd confided in her that I'd been abused before. I thought I could trust her. I had been taken advantage of. I had been used. I had been targeted by my Christian mentor extraordinaire.

As I replayed those instances in my mind years later, I realized there were other times too. Since they were less intense, I'd forgotten about them. I remember my grandfather's good friend, Mr. Graham, flashed his penis as a friend and I drove our bikes past his yard. I told my grandpa about that, and I don't remember going to see Mr. Graham again.

Time after time, my body seemed to be property of someone else. People touched me at will, without my permission, and never apologized for it. They assumed that I would never tell. They assumed that I would hold their secrets. And for a time, they were right.

Because we are silently (many times not formerly) sworn to secrecy, we cultivate this habitation and culture of silence. And it makes us feel like we are the only ones this has happened to; in turn we aid in creating isolated incubators of hopelessness throughout the globe. These incubators are places where pain festers and deficiencies and deficits become the normalized corridors where the fruit of sin and shame grow and develop. We become brooders, people who retreat mentally, and we persist in a world where our lens of love carries with it a film of filth and infection. It is not until we open up in our awareness and recognize that we are not alone that we can begin to heal from the shame, sharing our experiences, and seeking the support that we need.

Over the years, I've had men and women tell me their personal stories of molestation, and some of those accounts are so graphic and dehumanizing that they are fit for the movie screen. The intensity of some of the journeys these survivors have endured make own experiences seem like nothing. However, I didn't want this book to be a trauma matching experience, but to share enough stories to continue to remind everyone who read this that molestation can, and will, alter the lives of those who experience it, no matter how brief or longstanding. Abuse is abuse.

Contrary to belief in some cultures, molestation is not normal for everyone. Everybody is not molested at some point in their lives. But many have been. And until we talk about what has happened—what is happening right now—we'll continue to deny and diminish the experiences of those who have been affected by this trauma.

As survivors, we speak so we can all hear—and heal.

I want this book to be a part of breaking the cycle that has made molestation a taboo topic of conversation. In fact, I want to help victims of molestation understand that there are millions of adult men and women today, who were once boys and girls, that experienced the very thing that some of you dare not talk about.

So why don't we talk?

This forced silence happens primarily to protect the predators, as well as the people around us. Molestation implicates entire families. When the story is told, and the trauma is bought out into the light, not only are the abusers guilty, but so is everyone else who knew, but did nothing. And there is the guilt of those may not have known, but who are responsible for protecting and defending children, but could not save them. That includes parents, grandparents, sitters, and older siblings. The people who were supposed to keep us safe, that didn't. When we tell, our stories are perceived as accusations against every adult we know. When we tell, even as adults, we shushed back into silence. "Leave the past in the past," they say. But what if my past continually hurts and suffocates my present and future? The silence must be stopped. So, we share to stop the cycle of hurt. We don't want to create a society that is suspicious of every person that comes in contact with your child or grandchild, but we stop the cycle by making parents and care givers more aware, more vigilant about the possibilities of pain by sharing instances and experiences of those from all walks of life.

Beyond the physical pain molestation can cause, there is the psychological, emotional, and spiritual pain. When I begin to examine the core of the word "molestation," I found that the root word means to "bother, interfere with, or annoy." Molesters come, sometimes unaware, to bother, interfere, and annoy not only your body, but the purpose for which you were created. They come to intercept the plans that God has for you. They come to silence and suppress the pieces and parts of you, and your personality that would have enabled you to live out loud, and the passion that would have allowed you to love others, without questioning your identity and your sexuality. They came to disturb the essence of who you are and who you were made to be. Many may not believe it's that serious, but it is. Molestation is a spiritual act that impacts the body.

It may be hard to accept, but the truth is that abusers aren't thinking about the depth of the damage they cause. They aren't plotting and planning out molestation in their minds, thinking, "I'm about to destroy this child's life." The perpetrator's motives are selfish, and they pounce purely out of self-gain and self-gratification. They stalk the weakest, most vulnerable people they can find, like prey. They selfishly steal the innocence of the pure and virginal.

Molestation and childhood sexual abuse is as much about power as it is perversion. It's something about this level of control that heightens the abuser's sense of self. To have someone who they can willingly violate for pure enjoyment, sometimes because it was done to them, and without consequence is a dream come true.

Once a child is violated in this way, once their purity is taken away forever, doors are opened that can never be closed. Molestation causes significant, sometimes irreparable, damage to a person's identity, sexuality, and the total sense of self. This open door, or perversion, can often impact the personalities of victims, leaving their personhood in shambles. It changes them, in subtle and obvious ways. From depression to unexplained sexual promiscuity, victims exhibit behaviors and suffer from conditions, seen and unseen, as a result of their abuse.

For those of us who have lived through molestation, we know that is an indecent interception of the purpose, plans, and personalities of an individual, designed to silence or cause frustration to their minds, bodies, and eventually souls. Molestation has with it a vast agenda that penetrates the fullness of one's soul— as it impact is on one's mind, will, and emotions.

The encounters of molestation are so powerful that the experiences often leave deep tattoos of pain, devastation and complete incoherence on its victims. While these sexual predators sought to use us as pegs of brief enjoyment, they left stains. Stains that intercepted some of our purposes and pursuits, some that interrupted our happiness and joy, some that derailed our destinies. We hope that we can heal, and still become who we would have been had we never encountered those people that attempted to change us forever.

But can we?

OPEN WOUNDS

"Wounds that can't be seen are more painful than those that can be seen and cured by a doctor…"[5]

I understand fully the sentiments of Mr. Mandela about the impact of invisible wounds.

The wounds that childhood sexual abuse creates are undeniable. We can no longer neglect the internal intensity that the pain of molestation has caused so many people. And although women are largely impacted by the crime, and their stories are more widely known and shared, males are impacted nearly as much. This crime has no gender preference, nor a racial or socioeconomic one. The prevalence of molestation is flabbergasting.

---

[5] Nelson Mandela (in regard to the death of his mother and denial to see his son buried as he died in car accident while he was imprisoned for 27 years (age 44-71).

And while there are many other pertinent devastations that impact our society, this is a silent one that must be eradicated—soon. If we don't, generations of children will continue to be hurt and permanently damaged. The cycles of abuse will continue unless we confront the emotional and psychological disturbances of the perpetrators that cause this crime. If we don't, we will never impact change in a real way. We will never save the children who fall victim to these horrific acts somewhere, every minute of every day.

Later in this book, I will discuss, at length, some of the characteristics of a perpetrator, but I want to say up front, in short, there are only two reasons that we still deal with this issue: 1) Many perpetrators abuse because they are sick and are in need of healing and 2) Perpetrators abuse because they believe can get away with this. Bank robbers commit a crime, because they believe the institution has what they want. However, they rarely internalize the fact that there is a grave chance that they will be caught. Just like in the movies, either their plan goes array or the cameras they didn't plan on seeing them actually did. Abusers abuse, over and over again, because they can. They're never caught, since most people never tell. Especially if the perpetrator is a family member. If they are caught, often times, there are little to no repercussions. The depth of secrecy that exists regarding the topic of molestation in families, in church communities, within organizations, in schools, in every place where children are supposed to be kept safe, is deafening.

Let's look at the numbers and just a few of the countless stories of childhood sexual abuse:

Childhood Sexual Abuse at a Glance:

"1 in 4 girls and 1 in 6 boys are sexually abused before the age of 18."[6]

Author Bessel Van Der Kolk, M.D. wrote a riveting work in "The Body Keeps the Score: Brain, Mind, and Body in the Healing of Trauma" denotes that,

"More than half all rapes occur in girls below age fifteen. For many people the war begins at home: Each year about three million children in the United States are reported as victims of child abuse and neglect."[7]

While there are so many public stories of molestation and abuse, there are still countless others that have never been told. The statistics tell us that there are millions of people in the world whose stories of sexual abuse will never be told. These numbers represent the

---

[6] Finkelhor, D., Hotaling, G., Lewis, I. A., & Smith, C. (1990). Sexual abuse in a national survey of adult men and women: Prevalence, characteristics and risk factors. Child Abuse & Neglect 14, 19-28.

[7] Kolk, Van Bessel der, MD. *The Body Keeps the Score: Brain, Mind, and Body in the Healing of Trauma*. Reprint, Penguin Books, 2015. p. 20.

voiceless, the girls and boys who will never have a platform to tell what happened to them. Their pain will never be public or viral.

These are the incidents that were brushed under the couch. The ones that people suggested never happened. The ones that were "justified" because a girl was considered promiscuous, "fast" or "too grown for her age." The ones that never made the light of day. The ones, that still haunt the countless women and MEN who dare not discuss such a thing.

The Truth in Numbers

Childhood Sexual Abuse (CSA) is a global problem. Let's look at these statistics from around the world.

- The WHO in 2002 estimated that 73 million boys and 150 million girls under the age of 18 years had experienced various forms of sexual violence.[8]

---

[8] Geneva: World Health organization; Child maltreatment. 2014. Available from: http://www.who.int/topics/child_abuse/en/. https://www.ncbi.nlm.nih.gov/pmc/articles/PMC4311357/

- The highest prevalence rate of CSA was seen in Africa (34.4%).[9]

- Europe, America, and Asia had prevalence rate of 9.2%, 10.1%, and 23.9%, respectively.[10]

- With regards to females, seven countries reported prevalence rates as being more than one fifth i.e., 37.8% in Australia, 32.2% in Costa Rica, 31% in Tanzania, 30.7% in Israel, 28.1% in Sweden, 25.3% in the US, and 24.2% in Switzerland.[11]

- The lowest rate observed for males may be imprecise to some extent because of under reporting.[12]

- A review of studies from 21 high- and middle-income nations showed that seven to 36% of females and three to 29% of males reported being victims of sexual abuse during their childhood.[13]

- More than half (60%) of the sexual abuse cases reported that the incident took place before the age of 12.

- In a study conducted in Ethiopia among boys studying in high schools, the lifetime burden of sexual abuse was 68.2% and that of rape was 4.3%.[14] A study conducted in Hong Kong among college students on recall of sexual abuse before 17 years of age reported the prevalence of various forms of CSA to be 6%; these rates were higher in females. Majority of the participants reported being abused during their teens; the average age being 11 years.[15]

---

[9] Wihbey J. Global prevalence of child sexual abuse. Journalist Resource. Available from: Journalistsresource.org/studies/./global-prevalence-child-sexual-abuse .

[10] Ibid.

[11] Ibid.

[12] Ibid.

[13] Study on Child Abuse: India 2007. India, Ministry of Women and Child development Government of India. 2007. Available from: wcd.nic.in/childabuse.pdf.

[14] Haile RT, Kebeta ND, Kassie GM. Prevalence of sexual abuse of male high school students in Addis Ababa, Ethiopia. BMC Int Health Hum Rights. 2013 13:24. Available from: http://www.biomedcentral.com/1472-698X/13/24 .

[15] Tang CS. Childhood experience of sexual abuse among Hong Kong Chinese college students. Child Abuse Neglect. 2002 26:23–7. Available from: www.ncbi.nlm.nih.gov/pubmed/1186016 .

- Another study conducted in Mexico, reported prevalence of CSA to be 18.7% (58% in girls and 42% in boys).[16]

- In most (93%) of the cases, the perpetrator is known to the child (relatives, neighbors, stepparents, highly trusted people).[17]

That last point is startling, but it is a truth that we may struggle to accept, but one that we all know. Most childhood sexual abuse happens at the hands of people that children know. Children are being molested by the respected, the people who they love and should be able to trust.

Molestation is all around.

---

[16] Pineda-Lucatero AG, Trujillo-Hernández B, Millán-Guerrero RO, Vásquez C. Prevalence of childhood sexual abuse among Mexican adolescents. Child Care Health Dev. 2009 35:184–9. Available from: www.ncbi.nlm.nih.gov/pubmed/1899197518991975

[17] Department of Justice, Office of Justice Programs, Bureau of Justice Statistics, Sexual Assault of Young Children as Reported to Law Enforcement (2000).

Molestation in the Media

In 2006, phenomenal activist and leader Tarana Burke coined the term "#MeToo" which later sparked into a movement when actress Alyssa Milano tweeted it, asking other to share their stories. This was a collective effort to bring awareness to girls and women facing sexual abuse specifically in the workplace. In a CNN interview, Burke explained, "On one side, it's a bold declarative statement that 'I'm not ashamed' and 'I'm not alone.' On the other side, it's a statement from survivor to survivor that says, 'I see you, I hear you, I understand you and I'm here for you or I get it.'" The power of this movement has thrusted a plethora of stories that were buried for decades to the forefront of the conversation about those who have been molested by those that they once respected.

There are countless stories surfacing about individuals who were sexually violated by those in positions of authority. It has opened a conversation that until then, many were unwilling to share.

Renowned entertainers and executives like Bill Cosby, Harvey Weinstein, and Kevin Spacey, to name a few, have been publicly and legally indicted or convicted. As chronicled in the 2018 New York Times article entitled, *#MeToo Brought Down 201 Powerful Men. Nearly Half of Their Replacements Are Women*,[18] the paper generously detailed the accusation and charges that were brought against some of these men who were politicians from states spanning from Alaska, to Illinois, Arizona, Missouri, Florida, to Washington and Maine, North Carolina, Pennsylvania, to Texas and Wisconsin, to producers in mainstream Hollywood, to managing editors of major news outlets, to high school principals, to professors at elite universities, and even those at the sacred desk—evangelical pastors.

---

[18] Carlsen, Audrey. "#MeToo Brought Down 201 Powerful Men. Nearly Half of Their Replacements Are Women." *The New York Times Company*, 30 July 2019, www.nytimes.com/interactive/2018/10/23/us/metoo-replacements.html.

While it becomes sickening to learn of the gruesome actions taken against former staff members and colleagues and even budding actresses, it was even more devastating to hear about those made against children, both male and female alike. Actor Kevin Spacey faced allegations in this regard alongside Ohio State Representative Wes Goodman, as well as Bryan Singer, who in 2017, was brought up on sexual assault charges against a 17-year boy in 2003.

In recent years, stories of abuse inflicted by predominately white men, using their authority prowess in the marketplace to sexually and socially take advantage of their position as leaders, dominated the press. In each scenario, we've concluded that these men believed that they could use women, girls and boys, to be subservient to them and fulfill their sexual needs and get away with it. Not one of them was willing to face the consequential heat that their actions resulted in. Many are still denying that they committed crimes and maintaining their innocence.

Just as we thought the headlines and public trials involving childhood sexual abuse had reached their peak, in 2019, television media outlets exploded, airing accounts of intensive abuse by musical genius Robert Kelly of Chicago. The centerpiece of the conversation was a multi-day docuseries entitled *Surviving R. Kelly*. This *Lifetime* series detailed accounts of young girls, some from my hometown in Chicago, who desired careers in the entertainment industry and would do whatever was necessary to makes their dreams a reality.

Using his influence, Kelly preyed on these girls, creating a cult of innocent young women who willingly left their homes and families to be with him. Interviews with enraged parents are documented throughout the series, many of which hoped to bring their daughters home. Viewers watched night after night as these horrific, hard-to-imagine stories unfolded. There were sex tapes, nude and provocative images, chambers, forced lockup, and so much more that these girls were subjected to endure.

The docuseries,[19] produced by Dream Hampton, opened up conversations about the modus operandi of R. Kelly. Those of us from the Chicago area had heard rumors about some of his tactics and abuse for years. I remember various friends growing up who had older sisters that were involved with R. Kelly and meeting him at one particular local McDonald's restaurant. For the most part, there was not much mentioned in that series that we'd not heard in the streets before. While, I cannot personally verify the details in the documentary, I do know hundreds

---

[19] *'Surviving R. Kelly' Executive Producer dream hampton: 'I'm At War With R. Kelly'.* January 03, 2019. https://shadowandact.com/surviving-r-kelly-executive-producer-dream-hampton-im-at-war-with-r-kelly/

of women testified about how they too were molested by R. Kelly, someone they deeply respected.

What was fascinating to learn, but not surprising was something R. Kelly's brother shared during the docuseries. He has divulged information about how R. Kelly himself was molested by an older sister when he was still a lad. I would never excuse the behavior of a man who abuses, but I believe that we often skirt over the fact that boys and males suffer sexual abuse at nearly the same rate as girls their same age. Research suggests boys are less likely to confront what has happened to them, or to tell anyone because of the shame that becomes attached to their masculinity. Though extremely gifted, R. Kelly hid behind the pain and replicated what was done to him.

We must stop these cycles!
In recent years, there are several male public figures who are battling the challenges stemming from their

abuse publicly, and sharing their stories, including Keyon Dooling, Common, and Tyler Perry.

KEYON DOOLING

In 2012, as Keyon Dooling was starting his twelfth year as an NBA player for the Boston Celtics, something incredibly life changing happened—he was about to face the ugliest of his past. At 7, on a hot summer day, Dooling played at his friend's house. While there, he was introduced to pornography and abuse. A 14-year-old boy forced him to have oral sex with him. This day changed his life forever. The happy-go-lucky kid instantly became an angry, promiscuous boy. Not without struggle, Dooling persisted in school and held on to the dream of going to the NBA. He was an achiever and overcomer.

However, when he entered the stall of the public restroom and a homeless man groped his buttocks, it triggered the pain of Dooling's past. The incident was so intense that it sent him to a mental institution. This caused him to finally face the demons of his past.

These are some of Dooling's own words regarding the matter:

> I still hadn't told a soul what had triggered everything. Some part of me was still too worried about what people would think of me. I guess I was afraid that they would perceive me as weak, or damaged, or somehow at fault for what had happened to me in that apartment when I was seven years old.
>
> As hoopers, we never have time to process. We always have to keep moving on — to the next shot, to the next quarter, to the next city, to the next game. I spent 25 years of my life without a rearview mirror. I used alcohol and women and hoops to suppress all my emotions. But when I walked into that bathroom in Seattle, that was the trigger. Everything came rushing back. [20]

Speaking up and seeking help and healing, he said, "...has allowed me to hit levels of love that I didn't know I was capable of."

He went on to say:

---

[20] *Running from a Ghost* by Keyon Dooling. May 1, 2018.
https://www.theplayerstribune.com/en-us/articles/keyon-dooling-the-ghost

The thing that I realized when I went to therapy, it was like a physical relief, like the weight went off my shoulders... There's so many guys carrying their whole life experience around with them, and if they really want to soar, they got to get rid of some of that emotional baggage..."[21]

COMMON

Born Lonnie Corant Jaman Shuka Rashid Lynn, Common speaks candidly about his molestation. Recalling the incident, he says, "...but I felt a deep and sudden shame for what happened, and for what he kept trying to make happen, as if I had brought it all on myself." Sin is piercing. I'm reminded of Eve in the Garden of Life and when she was told not to eat the apple, she and Adam covered themselves with fig leaves out of shame." Common continued, "...

I didn't want to say anything, to anyone, and hoped he would just leave me alone, and go to sleep, which,

---

[21] Red Table Talk Season 2: Episode 2: *Molested As a Young boy: An NBA Star Breaks His Silence.* Facebook.com Show Starring Jada Pinkett-Smith, Willow Smith & Adrienne Banfield Norris. (5.5 viewers in November 2019).

57

eventually, he did once I fought back enough that he knew I was not going to touch him at all." [22]

During a movie filming rehearsal in 2017, Common suddenly recalled a time in his life that he had been sexually violated. He recounts it here, "Right there, it all came back to my mind as if one had suddenly inserted deleted scenes into that little movie in my head, scenes that I hadn't remembered or thought about before, scenes I couldn't even remember remembering. "[23]

Common continues,

> "All I can say really say about my memories is for whatever the reason, maybe out of self-protection, they remained inaccessible from me for decades, and now that they're back, slowly I've tried to sift through them, like old photographs found in a shoebox underneath the bed, to make sense of
>
> what it all means for me, and for the people in my life who I love, who love me, who had no idea that this had happened."[24]

---

[22] Common, *Let Love Have The Last Word: A Memoir*, Kindle Version. p. 115.
[23] Ibid. p.112.
[24] Ibid. p. 112.

In trying to distinguish the complexities of sharing a candid conversation with his mom nearly four decades after the molestation he says, " When I tell her about what happened, who exactly is talking: the ten-year-old boy or the forty-seven-year-old man he became; is it the child and son, or the man and father? Should she comfort me, or is it more important that I reassure and comfort her?"[25]

He goes on, "I don't know how to tell her. But I will, and I know love will see us through. I believe it."

Reflecting on what happened to him, Common adds,

> "I remember putting on the best face I could, but I was distant, perhaps as distance as another planet, feeling elsewhere within my own body, ashamed of myself and struck into silence. I said nothing to Brand, to Skeet, to my godmother—to no one, most certainly not my mother. I felt like I would never speak of it again, pushing it all out of my mind—or so I thought. More to the point, I buried it all in my mind, as deep as I could, hoping no one would see it or the shame that came along with it. And all of it stayed buried for decades."

---

[25] Ibid. p. 119.

As Common shares the battle in confronting this truth, I'm reminded that because of the complexity in rehashing all of it, many find it much easier to 'move on.' To continue with the weight of the pain, bearing it all themselves.

TYLER PERRY

After suffering beatings and being molested by three different men and a woman by the age of 10, Perry said, "I don't think I ever felt safe or protected as a child." While he was sure of his love from his mother and Aunt Mae, there was not much security in other places. Though incredibly intense, Perry speaks of how his gift of writing came when he would use his imagination to create new worlds to endure the abuse. He states, "...in the heartache, in the hell, in the pain, in my mind, whatever was happening, I can go and be somewhere else. As these things happened to me as a child, I could use my imagination and create these worlds and be there for hours… I'm a spectator in these worlds."[26]

Perry also suffered extreme beatings by his dad and survived several suicide attempts. One article reads, "Tyler says he was five or six years old the first time he was molested. While building a birdhouse with an adult male neighbor, the man put his hands in Tyler's pants. He says, "I'm thinking, 'What is this?'" And I felt my body betraying me, because I felt an erection at that age." Tyler says he later endured sexual molestation at the hands of a male nurse and a man he knew from church. "[The man from church] used God and the Bible against me to justify a lot of the things that were going on. It was so horrible," Tyler says. "And that was my first sexual experience, with this man performing oral sex.[27] Through it all, Perry was

---

[26] People TV: *Tyler Perry on Surviving Sexual Abuse As a Child, Retiring His 'Madea' Characters & More–10/04/2019 20,000 views…*
https://www.youtube.com/watch?v=r4saxuqYENs
[27] Ibid.

an overcomer. He states, "My childhood was a story of discouragement, belittlement, and unthinkable abuse, and yet I rose above. There is no way I could have found any kind of happiness, hope, or vision if my mother, Maxine, and my aunt Mae hadn't shown me the grace of God.[28] In speaking of forgiveness Perry said, "I had to. For me."[29]

A Quick Note on Forgiveness:

You'll notice that Tyler chose to forgive for himself, and no one else. This FREEDOM of forgiveness was a gift to himself. It didn't mean that he had to mend relationships with his abusers, allow them back into this life, or even have a conversation with them ever again. As Oprah has said, "just because you forgive

---

[28] Perry, Tyler. *Higher Is Waiting.* Penguin Random House, 2017. p. 14.

[29] Lane, Derrick. "Tyler Perry On His Childhood: "It Was A Living Hell"" *BlackDoctor*, 13 Sept. 2018, blackdoctor.org/tyler-perry-molestation-it-was-a-living-hell.

somebody doesn't mean you want to be *around them*."[30] There is truth here, particularly when it comes to forgiving your abusers.

Forgiveness is huge part of the process of healing from childhood sexual abuse, and it is a personal act. It is a gift to yourself, to ourselves. It's never for our abusers.

Keyon, Common, and Tyler are not the only celebrities who have shared their experiences with childhood sexual abuse. There is a plethora of public figures like Tisha Campbell, Oprah Winfrey, Whitney Houston,[31] Queen Latifah, Mike Tyson, Marilyn Monroe, Missy Elliot, Billy Holiday and many others who openly speak of their own experiences with sexual abuse.

Entertainers Vanessa Williams and Ellen DeGeneres are two other celebrities that I would like to highlight,

---

[30] Ibid. Posted on January 13, 2017Gemma Greene, BDO Staff Writer.

[31] This information was only recently revealed in her self- titled movies released two years following her untimely death.

who have publicly shared their painful recollections of their childhood sexual abuse.

VANESSA WILLIAMS

When she was 10 years old, Vanessa Williams was sexually molested by a female member of a friend's family. She details the experience in her memoir *You Have No Idea.*

Vanessa's Williams Experience:

"Nancy and I slept in the den on two sofa beds…I don't know how long I was asleep—minutes? Hours? But at some point, the accordion door to the den slowly opened and Susan crept in. I couldn't figure out why she was in our room in the middle of the night. Susan whispered, "Be quiet." She told me to get out of bed and lie down on the rug. I was confused. I looked over at Nancy, who was sleeping soundly. Are we going to play a game? As I tried to make sense of why this older girl wanted me to lie on the rug, Susan pulled down the yellow bloomers of my cotton baby-doll pajamas. "What are you doing?" I asked.

Don't worry—it'll feel good." I lay there paralyzed as she moved her tongue between my legs. What was going on? I didn't speak. She kept at this for I don't know how long. But it felt good, weird, and definitely wrong—all at the same time. She slid my bloomers back up and whispered:
"Don't tell anyone." I watched her as she crept back out. I climbed into my bed, still tingling at ten years old, trying to figure out what had just happened. Why had she done that? Was it something teenagers did to each other? Only girls? I thought it had to be something bad—why would she have

me told me not to tell anyone? I woke up the next morning feeling confused. We were heading back to New York and I couldn't wait to get out of that house and away from Susan.

My confusion and fears were evaporated by my family's grief. I pushed Susan's late-night visit to the back of my mind as we mourned for Uncle Artie.

For years I kept Susan's visit to myself.
My thoughts would always be overshadowed by Susan with her dark purple bedroom and the way she pretended to be the cool older kid to a ten-year-old on a summer vacation. Even, today, If I see a dark purple room, it just brings me back to that trip and I get a weird, sickening feeling in my gut.

I didn't really understand what had happened until I was in college. I was with my boyfriend, Bruce, and it just hit me, and I blurted it out: "Oh my God—I was molested!" It took me almost a decade to realize that I was an innocent victim and Susan was an eighteen-year-old predator. She had manipulated me the entire trip, just so that she could take advantage of me and I wouldn't speak a word of it. [32]

Reading about Vanessa's experience reminded me of much of my own. The level of manipulation and preying on younger women is sickening.
Most folks least expect older girls or women to defile their little girls, and most often leave their precious daughters lying in wait of harm and foul.

---

[32] Williams, Vanessa, and Helen Williams. *You Have No Idea*. Van Haren Publishing, 2012. pp. 103-105.

There are two details of her story that are common among abuse stories. One, there is a grooming process that predators use to gain access to other victims (which I speak about later in the book). Two, it's not usually until long after the encounter occurs that you understand the fullness of its impact. I will go into the effects of molestation in the next section of this text, but I want to note two things as I read more about Vanessa's story. One, she was silenced by the perpetrator, and two, which isn't laid out here, but in her book, she mentioned how she began to withdraw from her parents after the encounter that happened when she was 10. The effects of molestation can be devastating and long-lasting.

Ellen De Generes

Now 62 years old, talk show host Ellen DeGeneres revealed, more than a decade ago, how her stepdad molested her during her teenage years. He repeatedly groped her breasts pretending to check for breast cancer. Her mother had battled the disease, so at the time, a young, trusting Ellen didn't understand what was really happening to her. DeGeneres speaks about her need to be an example to girls and those put in these situations should use their voice to speak up. She regretted not having done so sooner but didn't want to hurt her mother or affect her happy marriage.[33] Ellen's story shows how trusted individuals are ideal and oft times, less assumed, perpetrators in sexual abuse. We also understand one again, the impact of silence.

---

[33] McDermott, Maeve. "Ellen DeGeneres Recounts Sexual Abuse: Stepfather Groped Me, Tried to Break into My Room." *USA Today*, Nov 16, 2019, 28 May 2019, www.usatoday.com/story/life/people/2019/05/28/ellen-degeneres-stepfather-sexually-abused-me/1256205001.

It feels as if new stories of victims who have been abused by celebrities and public figures surface every day. As more stories are shared, more victims feel empowered to come out of the shadows of their abuse and tell their truths. In the *Leaving Neverland* documentary, which premiered on HBO in 2019, two alleged victims gave jaw-dropping accounts of sexual encounters they experienced at the hands of popstar Michael Jackson. Marked with dark and sinister behaviors, together they recalled instances, in significant detail, of oral and anal sex, fictitious weddings, and love letters the singer gave to them. While the legitimacy of their claims has been highly questioned, both professed they were coerced not to tell anyone.

In 2018, Dr. Christine Blasey Ford, a Stanford University professor, sat in front of millions of viewers in the publicly broadcasted Senate Judiciary hearings in the accusation against then Supreme Justice nominee, Brett Kavanaugh. Dr. Christine Blasey Ford testified that Kavanaugh molested her during their high school years and while she could not recall all the details of what happened those several years before, she protested that he should not be confirmed as Supreme Court Justice as a result of the abuse he'd inflicted on her. However, Ford's testimony was not enough to keep him from gaining a position on the highest court of the land. Though not victorious, Ford won a battle many victims never win—she gained her freedom in speaking up. She wrote, "Coming forward was terrifying,' but I fulfilled my civic duty."[34] I would go further. Not only did Blasey Ford fulfill a civic duty, but she fulfilled a personal and spiritual one as well. She spoke up, she spoke out. And although 'justice'

---

[34] Johnson, Alex. "Kavanaugh Accuser Christine Blasey Ford Makes Rare Appearance to Accept Award." *NBC News*, 17 Nov. 2019, www.nbcnews.com/news/us-news/kavanaugh-accuser-christine-blasey-ford-makes-rare-appearance-accept-award-n1084696. *Accessed November 30, 2019.*

wasn't served because of it, she served as an example for me, even in the compilation of this project, and prayerfully for others to understand that your voice matters.

It Happens Everywhere

As these stories show, children and young people are molested and sexually abused in their homes, by neighbors, family members, and in social situations by friends and on dates. People with power lure victims with promises of fun, gifts, success, and even the love and attention every child wants and needs. But the sad reality is that children are subjected to sexual abuse in the "safe" spaces where parents and families send their kids every day, assuming that the adults there will protect their children as they would.

But perpetrators are there too and often times use their positions of power to violate their victimsAbuse is seen nearly everywhere. Here are some most notables areas:

Churches

In a *Washington Post* article, Boz Tchividjian, a grandson of Billy Graham and a former Florida assistant state attorney, said, "Sexual abuse is the most underreported thing — both in and outside the church — that exists,"[35] In recent years, countless accounts of children who have been sexually abused at the hands of clergy and church leaders have become more common, forcing us to realize that churches are not always the safe havens that we want them to be.

The *Houston Chronicle* newspaper published an article entitled "Abuse of Faith: 20 years, 700 victims."

---

[35] Pease, Joshua. "The Sin of Silence: The Epidemic of Denial of Sexual Abuse in the Evangelical Church." *Washington Post*, 31 May 2018, www.washingtonpost.com/news/posteverything/wp/2018/05/31/feature/the-epidemic-of-denial-about-sexual-abuse-in-the-evangelical-church. *Accessed October 1, 2019.*

On the face of the article, there were mugshots of 218 people who served as church pastors, deacons, and youth pastors who plead guilty of sex crimes against minors. From these incidents, over 700 children became victims with lifetime scars at the hands of people they trusted and respected. These predators used their positions and the promise of "safety" to lure vulnerable children to be self-gratified.[36]

In another instance in the church, a mother grappled with whether or not she would speak about a pastor who violated her daughter sexually. She battled with the fear of being ostracized for speaking the truth because of the impact her words might have. When considering whether or not she would suffer in silence, she understood what speaking out would me.

---

[36] Downen, Robert, et al. "Abuse of Faith: 20 Years, 700 Victims: Southern Baptist Sexual Abuse Spreads as Leaders Resist Reforms." *Houston Chronicle*, 10 Feb. 2019, www.houstonchronicle.com/news/investigations/article/Southern-Baptist-sexual-abuse-spreads-as-leaders-13588038.php. *Accessed October 1, 2019.*

She said, "… to doubt them [the pastors of her church] was to doubt God." Originally, she held the spiritual leaders of her church in high esteem, as did most of her community. However, her coming forward would have been viewed as a form of blasphemy.

Her actions would be risky. She did it anyway. While she braved the storm, there are many still suffering who cannot. [37]

Even outside of Evangelical churches, the infamous plight of the abuse scandal on the Catholic diocese is one that is still looming. The *New York Times* chronicled a litany of sexual abuse cases and allegations that involved the Roman Catholic church. With a plethora of cases listed, one discussed a case in Colorado involving 43 priests who violated 166

---

[37] Dias, Elizabeth. "Her Evangelical Megachurch Was Her World. Then Her Daughter Said She Was Molested by a Minister." *The New York Times*, 10 June 2019, www.nytimes.com/2019/06/10/us/southern-baptist-convention-sex-abuse.html. *Accessed October 13, 2019.*

children starting in 1950,[38] another in New York state that names 120 Catholic clergy members accused of sexual abuse, of which 115 were priests and 5 were deacons.[39] This is said to be the largest disclosure of the sexual abuse cases made by the Catholic church. Prayerfully, this will not only allow parishioners and parents to demand a new level of trust from spiritual leadership and to become more vigilant but will also serve as an opportunity to discuss molestation in a broader sense. Leaders must not abuse their authority and when they do, they must know that there are grave consequences.

---

[38] Stack, Liam. "Colorado Report Accuses 43 Catholic Priests of Child Sex Abuse." *The New York Times*, 23 Oct. 2019, www.nytimes.com/2019/10/23/us/colorado-catholic-church-abuse-investigation.html. *Accessed October 31, 2019.*

[39] Rojas, Rick. "New York Archdiocese Names 120 Catholic Clergy Members Accused of Abuse." *The New York Times*, 26 Apr. 2019, www.nytimes.com/2019/04/26/nyregion/archdiocese-priests-sex-abuse.html. *Accessed September 11, 2019.*

Clubs and Organizations

There are thousands more cases and accusations of childhood sexual abuse in trusted groups like *The Boys Scouts of America*, which now, have developed a track record of sexual abuse. The Boys Scouts of America (BSA) has tallied nearly 8,000 perpetrators of their leaders who allegedly sexually violated over 12,000 children since 1944. Memories of weekly meetings and outings are marred with details of depression as a result of the abuse. Though some of this information is readily available for public consumption today, the BSA has had a history of sweeping the issue of molestation under the rug. In 1972, a BSA executive wrote in regard to a scout leader perpetrator: "He recognizes that he has had a problem, and he is personally taking steps to resolve this situation."

This was after a perpetrator had acknowledged "acts of perversion with several troop members."[40] Robbie Pierce was a scout who got sick during a camping trip and had to visit the medical housing during the camp. It wasn't until years later during a discussion with camp buddies that he learned that he, along with several other boys, were fondled when they were made to get naked and had their penises groped when they sought medical attention.

In looking at the totality of the organization's history of sexual abuse, Pierce, "It provides pedophiles with access to boys...that has to stop."[41]

---

[40] Johnson, Kirk. "Boy Scout Files Give Glimpse Into 20 Years of Sex Abuse." *The New York Times*, 12 Oct. 2012, www.nytimes.com/2012/10/19/us/boy-scout-documents-reveal-decades-of-sexual-abuse.html?searchResultPosition=10. *Accessed October 1, 2019.*

[41] Baker, Mike. "Boy Scouts Seek Bankruptcy to Survive a Deluge of Sex-Abuse Claims." *The New York Times*, 18 Feb. 2020, www.nytimes.com/2020/02/18/us/boy-scouts-bankruptcy-sex-abuse.html?searchResultPosition=2&login=email&auth=login-email. *Accessed March 2, 2020.*

Now, we see thousands of lawsuits in which victims are suing the organization even though the acts were committed decades prior.

These claims have pushed organizations, like the Catholic Diocese and the U.S.A Gymnastics organization, to bankruptcy court due to monetary settlements that have been ordered to be paid to victims along with mounting legal fees. [42]

Another more notable organization is that of the United States Armed Forces. In 2018, the number of sexual abuse for women in the armed forces was up 50%.[43] Of the services, the Marine Corps had the worst record of sexual assaults against women, with an incidence rate of nearly 11%, followed by the Navy, 7.5%; the Army, 5.8%; and the Air Force, 4.3%.[44]

---

[42] Ibid.

[43] "DOD Sexual Assault Prevention and Response: What You Need to Know.2018 Annual Report on Sexual Assault in the Military" *U.S. DEPARTMENT OF DEFENSE*, www.defense.gov/Explore/News/Article/Article/1831742/dod-sexual-assault-prevention-and-response-what-you-need-to-know. *Accessed 4 Jan 2020.*

[44] Kime, Patricia. "Despite Efforts, Sexual Assaults Up Nearly 40% in US Military." *Military.Com*, 2 May 2019, www.military.com/daily-news/2019/05/02/despite-efforts-sexual-assaults-nearly-40-us-military.html.

In the more than 120 women who were stationed in Iraq, nearly half died of non-combat related deaths, and 25 of their deaths were by mysterious. Most of the suspicious deaths were deemed 'suicides' but sometimes are rapes. One source says, 1 in 3 women will be raped while in the military. Women of every hue and creed have become victims of "command rape." Command rape is where men in high command prey on new cadets. They ultimately use their power and authority to gain power and control mentally and ultimately sexually a female cadet.

There are a plethora of women who have been victims of command rape. One such is LaVena Lynn Johnson of St. Louis Missouri. To lessen the financial burden of college on her family, Johnson wanted to spend time in the armed forces before moving to

_____

California to become a movie producer. A stellar student with a huge heart, LaVena was a precious gym to her family.

One July morning in 2005, just 10 days before her twentieth birthday, LaVena's family received a knock at the door that would change their lives forever. Her parents learned that their daughter had passed away and that her death was under investigation.

After much probing and congressional involvement, Mr. Johnson was able to learn that his daughters' death was not the suicide they documented; there was more to the story. After examination of the autopsy, other account reports, pictures, and other colleague accounts, LaVena's family learned that her teeth were broken, her hips and joints were dislocated, there were bruises under her eyes, her nose was broken, there was a gunshot wound to her head, and chemical burns on her vaginal area along with parts of her vagina being cut away.[45] It's unmistakable that LaVena was murdered and raped. Still, in their pursuit of truth, the Johnson family continuously fight for justice for their daughter and the many others who are and were abused by the soldiers we all respect.

Schools

While conducting a random internet search with the phases "teacher molest student," nearly 3 million hits were swiftly tabulated. There are pictures of male and female teachers who are perpetrators, as well as male and female children from toddlers in daycare to teenagers in high school as victims. The information is endless.

In a San Antonio school, the male teacher is reported and accused of giving the student snacks and

---

[45] "The Silent Truth." *Youtube*, uploaded by 1091 On Demand, 9 July 2018, www.youtube.com/watch?v=5HGhaiJZNmc.

telling her to keep the molestation "their little secret." The victim in this case was 8 years old.[46]

A more infamous case that garnered media attention was that of Brittany Zamora, Arizona teacher. Here, evidence brought to light as a young white female teacher had sex with her 11 and 13-year-old students in her car and classroom, inappropriately touched students while in class and had a swarm of videos and text messages of indecent behavior.

During the sentencing phase of the case, one of the mothers of the students had these words to say: "Ms. Zamora lures these boys, earns their trust and then takes advantage of them purely to fill her own sexual desires,"

[46] Stunson, Mike. "Teacher Accused of Molesting 8-Year-Old Told Her to 'Keep It Our Secret,' Texas Cops Say." *The Star Telegram*, 5 Mar. 2020, www.star-telegram.com/news/nation-world/national/article240917941.html. *Accessed March 23, 2020.*

Later she states, "she used her position of power to molest a child."[47] These Arizona students were molested by a woman they respected.

Esther Miller, a former student and abuse victim, culminated an interview with these words, "Whether you're in the church pew, in the sacristy or on the blacktop on the playground, it is the same vibe," she added. "Whether it's the principal, the athletic director or the janitor, it is the same thing. Whatever power a child can have is stolen from them."[48] Miller speaks plainly of the violation of those in 'power' have over their victims.

They use their power to usurp the power of children, our world's most vulnerable targets.

---

[47] Burkitt, Bree. "Teacher Brittany Zamora Sentenced to 20 Years for Molesting Student." *The Republic*, 12 July 2019, www.azcentral.com/story/news/local/southwest-valley/2019/07/12/teacher-brittany-zamora-sentenced-molesting-student/1693827001. *Accessed August 21, 2019.*

[48] Stack, Liam. "Los Angeles Archdiocese Pays $8 Million to Teen Girl Abused and Kidnapped by Coach." *The New York Times*, 16 Apr. 2019, www.nytimes.com/2019/04/16/us/los-angeles-archdiocese-abuse-settlement.html. *Accessed January 5, 2020.*

What is dangerous about experiencing childhood sexual abuse at the hands of 'trusted' sources is the cyclical and expanding impact. One source says that 70-90% of those who participate in sex trafficking, were molested as children.

Their childhood sexual abuse experiences later became a gateway to the world of commercial sexual exploitation or sex trafficking. Human trafficking is "the illegal trade of human beings. It's the recruitment, control, and use of people for their bodies and for their labor. Through force, fraud and coercion, people everywhere are being bought and sold against their will-right now in the 21st century.[49]

The National Institute of Justice suggests that "preventing or intervening early in child sexual abuse will interrupt the path to sex trafficking.[50]

---

[49] A 21 Campaign, Inc. "Human Trafficking Is Slavery." *A21 Campaign*, www.a21.org/content/human-trafficking/gnjb89. *Accessed 21 Jan. 2020.*

[50] Darkness to Light . "Child Exploitation -Sex Trafficking." *Darkness to Light*, www.d2l.org/the-issue/child-exploitation-trafficking. *Accessed 13 Sept. 2019.*

According to the A21 website, sex trafficking is a $150 billion industry, with millions of slaves where only 1% of the people who are entangled in it is ever rescued.[51]

If we know nothing else, we know this—our children needed to be protected everywhere they go. And if they fall victim to abuse, their hurt and truth needs to be told and exposed so that these predators can be punished and stopped. We, as victims, need to be healed and set free. It's no easy task, but it's time to uncover the secret of sexual abuse.

One common theme I found in understanding my own story and learning about the stories of others is that speaking about our issues, particularly those that carry shame, brings freedom with it. In sharing her battle with alopecia, Representative Ayanna Pressley revealed her bald head and said,

---

[51] A 21 Campaign, Inc. "Human Trafficking Is Slavery." *A21 Campaign*, www.a21.org/content/human-trafficking/gnjb89. Accessed 21 Jan. 2020.

"I want to be freed from the secret and the shame that that secrets carries with it."[52] Though drastically different in nature, the same is true regarding the impact of childhood sexual abuse. The same sentiment is true in relation to this project. This book is about **freedom** from the secret and the shame of molestation.

Every person deserves to be free.

A predator can steal your innocence. But we cannot allow them to steal your freedom too.

FREEDOM

When prolific author and Christian speaker Joyce Meyer told her story of sexual and emotional abuse, she mentioned a fact that is worth repeating. She said, she aimed to tell her story not to bash her father, but

---

[52]Mitchell, Amanda. "Rep. Ayanna Pressley Revealed Her Bald Head in a New Video About Her Journey With Alopecia." *Allure*, 16 Jan. 2020, www.allure.com/story/ayanna-pressley-alopecia-reveal. Accessed January 20, 2020.

to become free. She went on to say, "you have to get it out in order to go over it." It's the truth that sets us free.

Childhood sexual abuse and molestation carry with it such shame that we never want to share our stories. We don't want to be blamed or stigmatized. In all of the confusion that comes with abuse, as victims, we lose sight of the fact that there was nothing that we could have done to cause this to happen to us. So, we hide and conceal. We cover. We stay silent. We convince ourselves that what happened to us didn't actually happen, or it didn't impact our lives as much as it has.

We persist through life without taking the time to deal with the abuse. We take the "I'll just sweep it under the rug approach." We try to forget since so much time has passed, and we should be "over" it. We don't want to risk appearing weak by bringing it up now, all these years later. And sometimes us coming forward will contradict the image we've created about ourselves. So, we leave it alone, covering up the wounds of our past.

However, what we also forget is that it is impossible to heal from something that you are unable to acknowledge. Your violation deserves to be validated. It deserves to be heard. Dealing with your abuse in your mind is not enough. Speak it so you can feel it. Speak it so that others can hear it. When we share, parents hold their children tighter and are more vigilant about their protection. Other victims feel less ashamed and feel brave enough to get the support they need. And you, ultimately, will feel free.
When we share and speak, we expose the wounds and allow it to heal. We heal.

In case you have not noticed it already, throughout this book, I will continue to bring you back to the importance of telling the stories of the abused. With this book, I want to create candid dialogue about those that have experienced childhood sexual abuse, and how it's spiritually and emotionally impacted those who have been victims of it. No topic is off limits. When it comes to sexual abuse, one act can cause a lifetime of issues if it is not understood and dealt with effectively. Every experience should be recounted and told so that, as victims, we can see ourselves in them.

Traumatic experiences leave traces. One author said of traumas, "they also leave traces on our minds and emotions, on our capacity for joy and intimacy and even on our biology and immune systems.[53] Understanding this, I know not everyone is willing to speak, or to face the monstrosity of abuse and its impact.

However, there are a brigade of men and women on the front lines that must tell the stories that others don't yet have the courage to reveal. We must

---

[53] Kolk, Van Bessel der, MD. *The Body Keeps the Score: Brain, Mind, and Body in the Healing of Trauma*. Reprint, Penguin Books, 2015. Prologue.

understand that we survived for a reason; this issue is much bigger than us.

One of my favorite authors, Randall Robinson, once wrote prior to standing up to give a speech on a college campus, "I look at the young people in the room. They cannot know how badly my generation has failed them."[54] When we don't find our voices, when we don't bring our dark stories out into the light, our molesters win. They continue to live their lives while we're left to pick up the pieces of ours. Previous generations did not tell.

They were too afraid, and too broken. They held those secrets. And the curse continued. This is a conversation that, until today, many of us dare not have.

---

[54] Robinson, Randall. *The Reckoning: What Blacks Owe to Each Other*. First Edition, Dutton Adult, 2002. p. 43

We cannot fail another generation by staying silent. It's time for us to be heard so we can heal individually then collectively.

Section Two

THE IMPACT

This book (alongside the online communities)[55] create a safe space where individuals and families can learn how to unravel the impact that molestation has on you or someone you might know. Growing up, lots of families stood by the notion, "what goes on in this house, stays in this house!" And I now know this mantra, this vow of secrecy, is why we're carrying so much hurt. Yes, it is important to have a sense of family, protection, and privacy. However, it's quite another issue when that privacy impacts one's emotional, spiritual, physical and mental health. We can't turn a deaf ear. In trying to "respect" someone's privacy, we may be turning the cheek and ignoring signs that someone we love has been victimized and is crying out for help. It is important for us to remain vigilant to heal our communities. As we dig deeper

---

[55] Website: www.molestedbutinvested.com and Facebook Group: *Molested But Invested.*

into the impacts of childhood sexual abuse in this section, my hope is that you walk away with a heightened sense of awareness. Whether you have been dealt the blow of molestation or you partner in life with individuals who have had such experiences, knowing how the weight of sexual abuse affects victims is essential to dealing with this issue. Our behavior is not just "who we are" or "acting out." What we do, who we are, is defined by what has happened to and around us.

Molestation impacts victims in different ways, but there are some traits that childhood sexual abuse victims commonly exhibit. Some may be obvious, and others can only be seen up close. The act happened long ago, but the impact can linger.
Sometimes, molestation and other abuses, have a way of marking its victims. Look closely.

THE MARKS OF MOLESTATION

We have learned that trauma is not just an event that took place sometime in the past; it is also the imprint left by that experience on mind, brain, and body. The imprint has ongoing consequences for how the human organism manages to survive in the present. [56]

There are seven characteristics that I believe are prevalent among those that have endured molestation. From my own experiences, and those of others who are close to me, I have witnessed these behaviors we all tend to share as a result of our abuse. These traits may show up in victims of other traumas, which is exactly why I wanted to share them in this book. *Molestation is a form of trauma.* When we understand the magnitude of what a childhood sexual abuse victim has endured, we can better understand the wounds that result from these experiences.

Being a part of a country that values scientific research and experimentation, I want to be clear: my

---

[56] Kolk, Van Bessel der, MD. *The Body Keeps the Score: Brain, Mind, and Body in the Healing of Trauma.* Reprint, Penguin Books, 2015, p. 21.

observations are not 'clinically tested'. However, I want to share insight on some common behavioral themes that I have witnessed over several years of life.

ONE: IMPENTRATABLE PRIDE

Pride is one of those things that can rear its ugly head as a result of so many life experiences. But I want to convey the impact that pride has on individuals who have suffered molestation because I believe it's so commonly misunderstood when it shows up in abuse victims. So much so, even they don't understand or recognize it. Pride's far reaching impact spills over to all the other areas that I will expound on below, but I do want to spend some time on this topic and talk about how pride enters and manifests in sexual abuse survivors.

The pride I speak about here is not the profuse gladness that comes in celebration of one's heritage, or the self-gratitude from accomplishing a   difficult task. The pride I cover here is a bit deeper. Pride is a spiritual disease that hardens the heart and is evident in all of your dealings with others. After sexual abuse, if we are not able to process the pain properly, we unconsciously do one of two things:

1). If the molestation occurs when we were children, it's possible that we become resentful as a result. We wanted to be protected, and we were not, so we stop looking for love and grow angry. Afraid to be vulnerable, we silently vow to never allow anyone else to get close to us again. We insist on taking care of ourselves, the best we know how. A wall of pride is built around us because we no longer want to be or even appear vulnerable.

Our hardened exterior reflects one who "has it all together. We aim to appear flawless, errorless. Sometimes, some us of overcompensating with our looks, we and dress to impress. We get applauded on the outside, hoping all along, nobody will detect what's going on inside.

Now, don't go around looking for well-dressed folks, pegging them as trauma filled. Or don't, stop your swag, I'm just bringing home an observation, I have made and wanted to share. ☺

2). If the molestation happened later in life, and we have kept the secret and not shared it, we move through life, pridefully, earnestly searching for people and places to impact. We want to live, but our secret holds us back. We can't be who we are FULLY called to be since we are still hiding something. Fearing judgement, we say nothing, and keep 'floating' around in life. Meanwhile, we are carrying a time-sensitive bomb of emotions that is waiting to explode.

If you were bleeding from your left knee right now, you could find a bandage, clean up, identify the source of pain, and move forward.

However, pride is a different type of wound, and one that a Band-Aid can't fix.

Pride is often undetectable by the person who possesses it. It is a silent assassin. Pride smothers the inability to ask for help. Pride is the invisible force that keeps individuals from being vulnerable enough to truly change.

Pride is "me" focused, me centered. Pride blocks your ability to see your need for God and any other person that could help you get past hurt. Pride when rehearsed enough, strongly resembles arrogance. The issue of pride is very prevalent with molestation victims.

You've decided in your mind that you won't be hurt like this again, so you build a wall that protects from hurt and shields you from help! Pride is a killer of all things. Pride kills relationships, dreams, greatness, everything that is meant for you!

Pride and denial are first cousins. When someone addresses the issue in your life, you deny, deny, deny.

To grow and change, pride has to be penetrated. It has to be broken. I want you to be honest, first with yourself.

Identify areas of your life where pride is present, and how it is hurting you and holding you back.

_____

_____

_____

_____

_____

_____

_____

_____

_____

_____

_____

_____

Another area I wanted you to understand in relation to molestation is identity.

TWO: CONFLICTED IDENTITY

A loss of identity is a common challenge that molestation victims struggle with. Typically, one of the first signs that a person is struggling with identity challenges is their indecisiveness. They may have difficulty with minute decisions such as choosing a restaurant, or bigger choices such as their sexual preference. This lack of decision-making skills leaves room for a plethora of issues. But there is one area that I must address first. It's a term I call *voicelessness*. Voicelessness is the inability to speak up and speak forth when necessary. Let's dig deeper.

Voicelessness

The most detrimental setback of molestation I believe is conflicted identity through a term I've coined as *voicelessness*. After a child is molested, chances are either: 1) they were told to not tell anyone (as we saw in many of the cases mentioned before) or 2) they told someone and were not taken seriously or 3) they believe their voices can cause harm to others so instead of 'inflicting that harm,' they choose to remain silent. Voicelessness is the act of not having a say, or the inability to use one's voice in a way that the individual believes it has the power to positively impact change. Voicelessness is no different from being mute. Those that are voiceless are incapable of making a decision; whether complex or simple, they are not certain about what they like, or how they like it. Their inability to make a choice is nearly crippling. They are often characterized—and paralyzed—by this muteness. Voicelessness is a result of trauma.

Speaking of such, I have always been fascinated with the renowned Dr. Maya Angelou. As a scholar, activist, orator, writer and poet laureate, it is clear why she had such an impact on American history, and even people all over the world. However, recently I learned that Dr. Angelou, though prolific in her craft, was mute for years following a traumatic incident of childhood sexual abuse. From the age of 5 until about 12 years of age, she spoke no words. After facing her accuser in court, he was brutally murdered. She believed her words were the cause of her perpetrator's death. And though her young mind couldn't understand that her words had nothing to do with the murder, she ceased to speak. Frustrated with her silence, her family shipped her off to Stamps, Arkansas. It was there that her grandmother introduced her to a woman with whom she developed her love of books. She also discovered the power of her own voice through written words.

Recently, I had a casual chat with my older sister, and we reminisced about random memories of our childhoods. I speak to her daily, but this time we delved into a conversation about something that was seemingly off topic. However, the veering in conversation was something that intrigued me that day. She mentioned how during our childhood, she would have to take me with her alongside her friends. Because she is six years my senior, there were many places and things she and her friends wanted to explore without me! It was funny because I often complained to my baby sister (who is three years my junior) because those same duties were later shifted to me. When I wanted to go to the mall, she was always the little sister that tagged along. For all the teenage reasons one could imagine, I hated it! Going further into the conversation, my older sister mentioned, "For a while, we thought something was wrong with you, because you didn't speak. You just sat there!"

We both chuckled and continued. She went on, "So, I took you with my friends, but you weren't any trouble because you never said a word!" We laughed profusely, but the contemplator in me logged this information in the back of my mind to be explored in the privacy of my own recollections. *Why was I mute? Had the happenings of my childhood shut me down? Was I experiencing something similar to Dr. Angelou and other victims of trauma?*

Similar to Dr. Angelou, I later became a writer and orator, but it took me a long while to understand the power of my words. And still, it was not without fight that I believed my words were worth hearing. Not until recently, I begin to explore my laidback nature and even my indecisiveness that shows up sometimes. *Was this always who I was? Or had experiences made me this way?*

I've learned, typically, that the area you struggle with the most, is the area you are called to have the greatest level of impact. Speaking and writing, using my voice, is a central part of my livelihood. Also, this was the same for Dr. Angelou. Angelou was able to pen millions of words in over 32 fully published books (including poetry, autobiographies, children's books, cookbooks, and religious analysis.) She contributed to even more books. Learning to use her voice garnered her a place on the Presidential program, when she recited of some of her work at the Presidential Inauguration of Bill Clinton in 1993.

As I learned about the characteristics of a molester and rapist; I now understand why the voiceless are attractive to the perpetrator. They are looking for vulnerable children who can be groomed. They seek those who are different, they seek those who like to be alone, and who stay separated from the crowd.

They prey on those individuals who maybe suffer from low self-esteem, those that may have low self-value. Those that exhibit an inkling of brokenness, are the ones in which they seek refuge. They seek the mute and voiceless ones.

In having that conversation with my sister, I had to wonder, had my quietness made me an ideal candidate for incidents to come?

MOVING BEYOND VOICELESSNESS

Maybe, like me, you were told to say nothing! And perhaps your immature mind subconsciously took that to heart. No matter how old you are, it is never too late to stretch beyond the person who was violated. It's never too late.

"Hurt must be heard before it can be healed."[57]

When you are able to heighten your voice, you not only let others know who you are and what you contribute, but you confirm and connect with yourself once again. You open the path to your own wholeness. To overcome voicelessness, and therefore gain an understanding of your identity, I believe it is important for us to discover, or uncover, the place where you can be heard. Where is the avenue that you can travel where you can express yourself the most authentically? Where can you reclaim your voice? It may not be with a microphone as a speaker, but it may be with a pen, and you can begin with a blog. Your voice might come through a paintbrush. Maybe you can sing.

Like Tyler Perry and even Tisha Campbell, maybe it's through acting and creating. Whatever you choose

---

[57] Texas Pastor Michael Phillips. Posted by his wife renowned psychologist Dr. Anita Phillips Instagram page.

does not have to be something that is made public, but perhaps your words are just for you to release. Releasing your voice, your words, and your thoughts is significant to the process of healing and understanding the essence of who you are. This can create an internalized value system that will ultimately positively impact those around you.

There are people, namely the people who hurt you, who are counting on your silence. In order for the cycle of molestation and trauma to cease, there must be an interruption. This interruption, this interception, is your voice and your true identity. If you remain silenced, you develop and contribute to the secret society of molestation. There must be a suicide of this secret society. If not, you keep a secret and after keeping it so long, it silently and spiritually kills purpose within you.

It silently strangles your dreams and your visions. It silently strangles your own hopes and dreams.

Maybe you did not say NO at the time of your molestation, but you have to chance to say NO to remaining silent. There is extreme power in saying NO! No, to no longer remaining silent! No, to accepting the secret! No, to agreeing with the wrong done to you! No, is a complete sentence.

Identify some areas where your voice has been silenced, and how you can reclaim your right to be heard. How will you begin to use your voice?

_____

_____

_____

_____

_____

_____

_____

The third area I want to highlight is a huge one, FEAR!

THREE: DEEP SEATED FEAR

Olympic gymnastics doctor Larry Nassar molested hundreds of athletes throughout his career. Now the woman who may have been his first victim reveals how a domineering coach created a climate of fear that enabled sexual abuse:

> Today, she wears a metal knee brace from old gymnastics injuries. Physical pain is a part of her everyday life. Then there are the psychological scars. "People don't understand how many broken girls it takes to produce an elite athlete," she says, delivering the haunting words with the perfect posture of a gymnast. "A coach can easily go through 300 girls, or more."[58]

The girls who became Nassar's victims were full of fear. They'd been broken by their coach, broken by the pressure of becoming world-class athletes, broken by the criticism, all while being distanced from a "normal" life, school, family, and friends. All of that brokenness made them vulnerable to a man who was supposed to

---

[58] Pesta, Abigail. "An Early Survivor of Larry Nassar's Abuse Speaks Out For the First Time." *TIME MAGAZINE*, 18 July 2018, apple.news/AdsblWKr_Rvqos4njxjmZjA. *Accessed July 4, 2019.*

be there to help them, to protect them. Instead, they too, were violated and molested by someone they trusted and respected.

I was with a friend as we walked to Trick or Treat with our little children. We discussed about our mates, and she shared something very profound with me. She said, 'You either make choices out of love or you make choices out of fear." That stuck with me. And the statement is something I completely agree with. Every choice we make either comes from love, or from fear. Even with this project, initially, I didn't want to do it because of fear. Fear of what folks would say. Fear that the topic wouldn't be embraced. Fear that there would be a lot of, "I told you so!"

And just as Nassar created a culture of fear for hundreds of gymnasts, it was evident that he understood the crippling impact of what it does.

Fear is the most debilitating emotion anyone could ever experience. To image that a 60-year-old man who was sexually abused is still gripped with the fear of a threat that happened at five years old seems outlandish, but in reality, is more likely to be true than not. We all have fears, especially when we've been sexually abused or any sort of trauma.

Fear is an illusion that robs you of your truth. Fear, by definition, "is the anticipation of the possibility that something unpleasant will occur." As I have matured, I understand that often individuals who suffer from various levels of trauma are often prideful people. Fear is many times disguised as pride.

You have spent so much time not being in control of what happened to you that you work hard to ensure that others will never gain that level of control over you again.

I mentioned this before but want to herald it again. In the midst of that you create a partition, to protect your soul. But in turn you have erected a fortress around your heart. Those that desire to come in your life without motive are left on the outside of the fortress and are unable to penetrate your heart and life to give you the love you so desperately need and deserve. You've declared, "I'll never be hurt like that again!" So, out of fear you have shielded your heart, but also made it impenetrable to accept and receive love. I understand it fully. I was there too!

Internally, because of your fears, and you don't believe you are smart enough, connected enough, or don't have enough money to pursue the fullness of who you were meant to be.

Fear is gripping. However, fear has to be confronted. This confronting doesn't have to be done in a hostile way, but it must happen. I think most of us just want to be nice people or at least appear that way. We never want to come across as "the mean one." Most of us don't aim to be agitators.

We much rather go along and get along. We don't want to stir the pot and be problematic. We don't want to get anyone upset. We don't want to be deemed a troublemaker. We don't want to upset the status quo. We want to remain 'politically correct'. We want to just "keep living", even if we are dying inside.

Fear is an illusion. It creates with it conversations that suggest because it happened so long ago, we should simply, "Get over it!" We should leave the past in the past." I get it, I do! Some past things and people belong there, but your freedom doesn't.

We have to disable the power of fear because it has the ability to spread and infect like cancer. Often fear in one area will silently stifle you in other areas. It's like fear has what I call, an *umbrella effect*. It has one handle, but its spokes reach violently into other **all** areas of your life. It's overarching impact becomes the foundation upon which your life is lived.

UMBRELLA EFFECT OF FEAR

Moving Beyond Fear

If fear (and pride) isn't checked, it, in turn, turns into subtle bondage that becomes the foundation and bedrock of your life. Fear becomes the lens from which you operate and see the world. Fear creates insecurity of identity; it creates an insecurity in your sexuality. Your ability to properly relate to other people is questioned, even by yourself. The fullness of your identity is unseated, unhinged. Confronting fear allows you to harness peace in every area of your life.

I've always been afraid of deep water. Last summer, I came to a point in life where I was determined to eliminate all of my fears, I knew that learning to swim in deep water was the final fear that I was determined to conquer. I wanted to learn to swim in the deep end of a pool. I couldn't teach myself, so I decided to hire my kid's deep-water swimming coach as my own. In preparing for my sessions with my instructor I researched the concept of buoyancy. Buoyancy, I learned, meant "something or someone that is not depressed, something or someone that is light, airy, not heavy." To be buoyant means "something that is unsinkable." I showed up for my first lesson hoping this concept of buoyancy wouldn't fail me.

I got into the pool the first time. We practiced some basics, and then with each lesson, my instructor encouraged me to do a little more. Though the waters raged around me, by the end of 8 sessions, I was no longer submerged in the fear of what was around me, but I learned the proper techniques of breathing, or releasing and movement through treading, and various strokes to survive and ultimately thrive in something that was meant for my enjoyment. After a few sessions, I was more buoyant than I ever knew. When I allowed my body to relax, I stopped pushing against myself out of panic and fear, I could float if I needed to. While I still don't desire to be thrown in the middle of the Pacific Ocean or anything, but in my 8ft pool, I was unsinkable.

Swimming in deep waters was something that I had feared for years. It was a similar fear that had seeped in during a molestation encounter and drowned me and robbed me of years of memories with my children and other family. In fact, fearfulness had become a part of my personality. It impacted my conversations, and my ability to create, foster, and retain meaningful relationships. Fear has far reaching affects. We must face it, fight it, and find ways to keep fear from drowning us, when we are really unsinkable. The fact that you are reading this, let's me know you are buoyant too.

Dig deep. Identify ways that fear is holding you back. Thing about areas that you have considered yet haven't progressed. How will you face and fight each of those fears?(Ex: I'm scared of...I'm afraid that....)

_____

_____

_____

_____

_____

_____

_____

Cultivating meaningful relationships is also, sometimes, an area of challenge for those who have experienced the trauma of molestation.

FOUR: LACK OF MEANINGFUL RELATIONSHIPS

Regarding the topic of trauma, one author said, "...having been exposed to family violence as a child often makes it difficult to establish stable, trusting relationships as an adult."[59]

Another time he said it this way,

> Trauma, whether it is the result of something done to you or something you yourself have done, almost always makes it difficult to engage in intimate relationships. After you have experienced something so unspeakable, how do you learn to trust yourself or anyone else again? Or, conversely, how can you surrender to an intimate relationship after you have been brutally violated?[60]

I truly agree. Trust, be it of yourself or others, after the trauma of molestation is one of the hardest obstacles to overcome.

---

[59] Kolk, Van Bessel der, MD. *The Body Keeps the Score: Brain, Mind, and Body in the Healing of Trauma*. Reprint, Penguin Books, 2015, prologue.

[60] Kolk, Van Bessel der, MD. *The Body Keeps the Score: Brain, Mind, and Body in the Healing of Trauma*. Reprint, Penguin Books, 2015, p. 13.

Once the act of molestation has occurred, I've seen either one of two behaviors result as it pertains to relationships. Some individuals become extra clingy and are so "needy" to the point that they can't operate in life without an intimate relationship and therefore suffer deeply, if one is not present. Often, if that relationship is present it is riddled with control and possessive type behaviors. If left unchecked and unhealed, these individuals often become a part of an abusive relationships or in many instances are the abusers in these relationships.

Van Bessel der Kolk continues:

> *After trauma the world becomes sharply divided between those who know and those who don't. People who have not shared the traumatic experiences cannot be trusted, because they can't understand it. Sadly, this often includes spouses, children, and co-workers.*[61]

This division seen, even in the most intimate relationships are incredibly tragic.

---

[61] Ibid. p. 18.

On the other hand, there are those individuals who, because of the violation of the sexual encounter, have obliged to steer away from relationships all together. They have decided that they are better off by themselves. They are committed to being as removed as possible from intimate relationships. When they do in engage in relationships, they only engage at surface level. They are pretty emotionless in their dealings. Though they don't intend to show up this way; their encounter(s) of abuse have transformed them into this. Because of the need to survive, we've had to suppress those feelings of anger, hate, abandonment, and love. Their emotions got swallowed in the mix of the trauma and the attempt to recover. This survival mechanism keeps victims at the surface, and no further. However, we have learned through research that surface relationships are not stable. The durability of these relationships is not long standing.

Emotional connection is essential for any relationship to last and flourish. However, if deep connections are formed before proper healing takes place, most often they become unhealthy soul ties. Unhealthy soul ties can form with new relationships if one party is unhealed, and unhealthy soul ties can also form with past abusers. Let me explain further.

Soul Ties

All connections are spiritual. Spiritual connections reach beyond surface level and are attachments of the soul. The soul is one's mind, will and emotions. Soul ties, therefore, are ties that impact your mind, your will and your emotions. Some soul ties can come through sexual encounters. Soul ties are those intense bonds that come through those who spend intense amount and time together through conversation and/or physical intimacy. There are healthy soul ties and there are unhealthy ones.

Healthy soul ties are typically seen in healthy and strong marriages. They are the ties that bind unions. They are seen in healthy friendships and other relationships. However, the unhealthy ties and other intermingling, if not careful, can create within them measures of bondage.

Example of an Unhealthy Soul Ties

You've dated someone for more than 4 years. There is a deep disagreement in the relationship and you all suddenly part ways. A year passes and you have yet to resolve the disagreement. You often have dreams about them. Everything you see reminds you of them. Because you have spent massive amounts of time together exclusively, you sound like them when you speak, and some of your mannerisms even resemble theirs. Another year passes and you've now entered another relationship.

You are pressed forward and have even started a family. Your marriage is happy, but every so often you have reoccurring thoughts of that last relationship. Unwarranted angry seeps into the new relationship and begins to impact it negatively. You have yet to understand why things have shifted in a negative direction and are soon headed for a divorce.

The previous soul connection caused the future relationship to go awry. This happens because many times, we have not taken the necessary steps to move past soul ties and in turn keep infecting upcoming relationships with the debris of the past. If you do your research, I'm sure there are a plethora of sources on the topics, but I wanted to insert these brief thoughts. The overall point is: The past must be dealt with, even severed in order for true peace to happen in the new relationships. Many times, those that are looking to be married, think marriage will heal all of their wounds.

Marriage only amplifies the bleeding. **Steps to overcoming soul ties:**

> 1. Take time to heal from one relationship before entering a new one.
>
> 2. Be honest with God through prayer and the other party in the relationship about how you are truly feeling. When issues are exposed, they lose their power. What's hidden can be healed. Address your pain.
>
> 3. Break all ties with from the individuals and entities that caused the bondage. This includes getting rid of old articles of clothing, gifts, etc. We can't take the old into the new.
>
> 4. Identify people that you know, trust and respect that you can share with during your times of struggle. Be sure they don't coddle you but keep you growing and accountable. Remain transparent.
>
> 5. Stay connected with healthy relationships that can serve as examples of how you can progress.
>
> 6. Never make peace with the struggle. Keep fighting to get stronger and stronger until ties are broken and have no power of you—how you feel, think and act.

Breaking soul ties is setting yourself free, and freedom is something that must be practiced. I remember a person I knew who was wrongfully convicted of a crime in Illinois who was suddenly released in 2003.

After spending 14 years in lock up, he said that because he had spent all those years walking with a chain around his ankle, he struggled with his new freedom, in every sense. Once he was released, he would walk with only one foot a few inches in front of the other, as to not trip . Though he was no longer in chains, his mind and body had not caught up with his true freedom. Now, he has to consciously and intentionally tell his mind that he has transcended his chains. Eventually, the entire memory of the bondage will be destroyed. Be patient with yourself. Freedom must be practiced.

Former relationships can be places of wisdom and growth as we move on with our lives. However, if we don't properly and consciously break all ties, they can negatively impact our lives, preventing us from moving forward and creating true bonds with those who are called to bless our lives and us theirs.

The Spirit of Comfort

Another relationship issue that is prevalent, especially among molestation survivors, is an introduction to what I call the spirit of comfort. This spirit is subtle, sly, and long-lasting if not forthrightly confronted.

My aim was not to be too religious throughout this conversation, but the only way I know to explain this is head on. Follow me.

For this topic, the spirit of comfort is often evident when the perpetrator has been molested and consciously or subconsciously forms a bond with their victim in an effort to find a sense of commonality. This is part of the grooming that happens. If a perpetrator can get a victim to trust them, by appearing emotionally wounded and vulnerable, it is easier to lure that person in and gain control. Once the victim trusts, the sexual abuse ensues.

Now they are bonded by the brokenness of molestation. This bond creates a level of comfort that ultimately seeks to control its victim.

Understanding the Spirit of Comfort

This spirit can be evident in any trauma or relationship. The spirit of comfort is a place. It's a place that seeks out the yearnings of your innermost desires. It's the place that massages the wounds of its victim instead of seeking to help heal them. It's a place that feels tremendously and exceptionally safe. It's the place that makes its victims feel they've finally achieved a sense of enlightenment. This place entices you to finally be yourself. It seeks to comfort you, so you don't have to put on parades or shows, just plainly be you. It's the place that desires you to feel the most understood. It's the place that provides you set of blinders. This place offers a false security.

This place feels like the perfect,-its-too-good-to-be-true kind of relationship. The spirit of comfort is very cunning. It looks right. It feels right. The comfort seeks to numb you to reality and creates a fantasy-type world. It is a detrimental place and is a dangerous place.

The spirit of comfort is a place that seeks to push you to commit spiritual suicide. Somehow killing the essence of who you are that melts into the person and personality of that person who is attached. It's a place that takes years to overcome. It is a place that sought you out because of your wounded, patched up, but unhealed past. This place makes you believe everybody else is wrong and you are right. But eventually, comfort will coerce you into letting your guard down. It's a place that slowly chips away walls that once protected you. This place leaves you vulnerable. It leaves you open. It's a doorway that provides the foothold to the enemy to champion causes of victory in your life. It wants to connect and attach at ALL levels. When the phone isn't enough, the comfort is there. When the social media outlets aren't enough, the comfort is. This dangerous place, for many, usually leads to sexual perversion. Many incidents of incest and homosexuality happen at this place. It's not because you were born this way, in many ways it is unfinished business that you have yet to accomplish in your soul that it now has entangled itself with another and found 'peace'.

The spirit of comfort is a type of soul tie that seeks to dominate and control and isolate. Manipulation is usually a tenet that coexists where the spirit of comfort operates. The spirit of comfort seeks us out when the default or unhealed spaces in our lives are not agitated. When the spirit of comfort is present, we only long for or seek relationships that will enable us in this stagnate stage. We tend to resist the relationships or situations that challenge the default settings (unhealed), and usually come to offer us healthy love, support, and security. This is where we must take our power back.

It's time that we reformat your entire system! In order to properly reformat your system, you have to resist being comfortable in all aspects of your life. You have to be willing to come away from those deceitful, unhealthy, familiar spaces, and into healing. You don't need to hide where it is dark and dangerous. That is not safety. Healing is safety. Wholeness is safety. Come out of the 'comfortable' spaces. You're worth it.

Identify and list the relationships in your life that you know lack meaning or are unhealthy for you in any way.

_____

_____

_____

_____

Do you believe you are you bound by the spirit of comfort or a soul tie? How do you know?

_____

_____

_____

_____

What are some practical ways you can shift that now? Remember, honesty is most important.

_____

_____

_____

_____

_____

_____

_____

_____

_____

FIVE: ISOLATION & CONTROL

The 5th mark of molestation I've hinted at during our time here, is isolation and control. While isolation and control are two separate entities, they often coexist. Hence, I want to address them in this section synonymously.

The Spirit of Isolation

Isolation can be a drawback from a soul tie or a natural response to the trauma of molestation. Instead of pushing forward in forming new bonds, some of us retreat to spaces of comfort. It may be comfortable to be alone or often distant from others, physically or emotionally. Or maybe like Tamar, your isolation has been forced upon you.

During these isolated phases, we focus solely on internal needs and desires. We protect ourselves. We close off from others. Often, when we do enter relationships, we selfishly fulfill our own desires and lack empathy and understanding of others.

We turn inward and choose to believe the negative thoughts that are cast in our minds. The lies of our experiences tell us that we are unworthy, damaged, and unlovable. And we believe them. This is tied largely to our inability to form intimate bonds, as previously mentioned.

The Spirit of Control

The controlling spirit seeks to dominate. When a person is sexually abused as a child, their power is taken from them. Victims, as adults, tend to either be overly controlling themselves, or easily dominated. Those that fall in the latter category are highly susceptible to controlling people and authority figures who leverage control to abuse in other ways.

This dynamic is familiar to the abused adult, since it replicates the childhood experience. Once a victim experiences this, they believe that this is the formula for all "real" and "true" relationships. As they grow, they remain trapped in it. Those who operate with controlling spirits, hope to isolate their relationship with you. These people are threatened by the closeness of others to you. They want to be your "only one!" The spirit of control takes on a life of its own. It wants you to itself.

When a victim leans towards the opposite end of the spectrum, and becomes the dominant one, they seek positions of power to allow them access and authority to control as much as possible. They are supervisors, they are politicians, and pastors. They even seek romantic relationships and friendships in which they are older, and more experienced. They don't follow well, believing that following anyone in some way disables their control.

They don't remain part of organizations and institutions very long, and if they do, they create a subset of the group, forming their own segmented society which allows them terrain to dominate.

Both abused, the victim who allows themselves to be controlled, and the one who seeks to control, often share the same space. This is often how cults are formed. Most cults and underground organizations lure people in because they have successfully isolated potential members from their families and communities, in turn creating their own communities and ways of living.

Survivors of cults often speak about how initially, in the recruitment phase, the leader made them feel special in some way. They were courted, wooed, flattered, and adored in the beginning. The perpetrator positions the relationship to where you believe that only they are the 'truth'. They create a form of isolation.

They learn of your greatest needs and desires and begin to supply them. This, in turn, creates a sole dependence on them more than anyone else. Their goal is to gain first place in your life. After the trophy (your heart) is won, they pounce. Survivors recall that, once they were inside, they soon realized that they weren't special at all. Once the wooing process was over, they quickly discovered that they were one of many. Trapped, the abuse and control ensue. Most times you are in so deep that you can't see the truth of what you are experiencing. If you are lucky enough to escape, you've had to rebuild your life on broken pieces. The relationships you've abandoned for the one main prize, are all gone. The family you've sacrificed is nearly in shambles.

Many times, the bondage that comes with isolation and control takes years to finally recognize.

Control was a major factor in my molestation. When I was abused by my mentor, she made sure that she held power over me from the very beginning. As I think back, when the relationship was starting to form, she pursued me in such an aggressive way that as to push the other relationships in my life at the time to the periphery. She sought, successfully, to make herself the center of my world. She wanted to control me, to convince me that she could fulfill a need that no one else could, and to be the only person I could trust and seek for counsel. Because I am a loyalist to the core, I fell for it.

For instance, I was the first in my immediate family to pursue graduate studies. I didn't know about seeking funding, assistantships, and other types of resources that would make my graduate school experience a better one. My molester knew that I was naïve, introverted, and overwhelmed with information, and positioned herself as my guide and filter for all the information she knew could help me. She leveraged her knowledge and connections to manipulate me and, in a sense, she controlled the trajectory of my life at that time.

I didn't recognize her tactics to control me until years later. It was subtle to me and done under the guise of trying to be a helpful resource. Allowing myself to be controlled, manipulated, and silenced in this way was a pattern of behavior that continued for years, well into my adulthood. The entity shifted, but the reality remained the same. I went from a deeply controlling relationships to severely controlling church. The cycles don't stop until you confront it. Many victims of childhood sexual abuse find themselves in this similar cycle—trusting the wrong people and giving their power over to someone of perceived authority or influence.

If you have had this experience, I want you to know, all is not lost.

You can rid yourself of these isolating and controlling relationships, as well as the shame that comes with them. The first and most powerful step is to recognize these truths and move forward. It's possible. I'm proof.

Identify any relationships that are rooted in isolation or control. If you can't see it yourself, survey close family and friends to help you in this process. Remove any offensive attitudes that may hinder you from seeing the truth.

_____

_____

_____

_____

_____

_____

_____

_____

_____

SIX: LACK OF VISION & LIFE CLARITY

Trauma clouds your vision. It inhibits your perceptions. Without the violation of molestation, many of us would know of all the right things to say and do. We would be clear on where we are headed in life, and how to get there. If those seeds of doubt, fear, a lack of security, a lack of self-worth, and a lack of love had never been planted, we'd be fully flourishing by now. But they were. So, we consistently wrestling with inner turmoil regarding the truth of our identity and purposes in the earth.

Molestation can often blur the lines of identity. As previously mentioned, once the act of molestation occurs, depending on who and how the act happened, it can leave with it questions about oneself. For instance, why did this happen to me? Many times, victims evaluate themselves based on what we have experienced.

Did something about me say I was "easy"? Was I not attractive enough to be respected and therefore molested?

If the gender of the person was the same as victims, often the victim can deal with issues of homosexuality and therefore have an affinity towards the same sex. And while they most times are not interest in same-sex relations, because in most instances the molestation was their first sexual experience, it becomes the "teacher" for all subsequent experiences. Or their first experiences disgusted them so, that they turn to the same sex for love and nurturing.

Marie Osmond speaks of this same issue of sexuality of during a recent interview. She says:

> "Marie Osmond says she questioned her sexuality after being sexually abused at a young age. "I share my life here, but when I was 8 or 9, I actually thought I was gay," she said . "And the reason is because I had been sexually abused to the point that men ... they made me sick. I didn't trust them; I didn't like them."

> The singer continued, "… there was a point in my life that I thought, well, I had so many body issues and different things, and I was looking at women and I thought, 'Well, why am I looking at women? I must be gay.'" [62]

When the fundamental question of "Who am I?" is not answered or is insanely blurry, sexually or otherwise, we spend our lives trying to find the answer. Many of us get hurt and confused while on this quest.

Molestation intercepts a victim's identity, at one of the most critical and vulnerable times of their lives—childhood. Children are wide open, mentally, spiritually, and emotionally. Everything they hear, see, and experience influences who they will become. When the sexual abuse occurs, it creates a whirlwind of emotions and leaves the victim perplexed. Often, a life of chaos ensues.

---

[62] Todisco, Eric. "Marie Osmond Says, 'I Thought I Was Gay' After Being Sexually Abused: Men 'Made Me Sick.'" *People*, 22 Oct. 2019, apple.news/APbbFIoNFSxS_kfCu9QPNsg.

Instead of maturing into their own person, the victim latches on to the vision of others in hopes of finding a sense of stability and validation. A victim's mind says, "if I was chosen as the one to be molested, I must not be valuable. I must not be worthy. Nothing valuable can come from me." Silently, this becomes their life mantra. There is the level of negative self-image that develops, coupled with regret. Victims deeply desire more. They just don't know how to get from here to there.

Individuality and purpose are likened to the specificity of our own fingerprints. What is yours is yours. You can't abandon your assignment because of the abuse. If you don't understand the fullness of who you are, when you are misused, you believe the purposes in which were used is the essence of your truth. Hence, there are many individuals who were molested that have become promiscuous.

They were used for sex and therefore believe that being used for sex is their purpose. Their purposes were prostituted like women and men in the night. However, they are so far from themselves and the repercussions of the abuse has become their only hope.

This section may have been hard to read, but I wanted to me honest with struggles in relation to identity. These are some stains that abuse has left on our spirit, but we can wash them away. Stay with me. We can become new. We can all overcome.

Identify the areas in your life where you feel unclear. It could be a broad question, such as your lives' purpose, what you were created to do or to be, or something specific, such as your sexuality. You want to begin to get clear on where this confusion has set in as a result of your abuse, so you can begin to find your way to healing.

_____

_____

_____

_____

_____

_____

_____

_____

_____

_____

SEVEN: ARRESTED DEVELOPMENT

Lastly, I want to chat briefly about a biological impact of trauma. Scientific studies are now investigating traumas and their correlation to arrested emotional, mental and/or psychological development. While I won't layout the detail specifications of the scientific research here, as it is quite vast, I do want to ensure you understand that abuse can often inhibit your emotional and developmental growth and leave you stuck at the age of your trauma.

I often refer to myself as a "late bloomer" when, in reality, much of my life was paused as a result of being molested. This delayed, or arrested, development, was caused by the childhood sexual experiences that I encountered. One element of research suggests that not being touched enough as an infant could delay the growth and development process. However, being "overly touched can also create this same arrested development.

Another school of thought, details how childhood sexual abuse and other traumas can actually cause brain damage.[63]

Yet another researched said it this way, "Perhaps childhood abuse has arrested psychosocial development, leaving a "wounded child" within the adult."[64] I'll explain, when you are sexually abused, you are often stuck or 'arrested' at the age of the event. Let's say you were developing healthily at the age of 7, then at 8, the abuse began, and continued until you were 18.

---

[63] In citing a portion of one study, the author writes, "…the right hemisphere of abused patients had developed as much as the right hemisphere of the controls, but their left hemispheres lagged substantially, as though arrested in their development. These studies suggest that child abuse may alter development of the left hippocampus permanently and, in so doing, cause deficits in verbal memory and dissociative symptoms that persist into adulthood." Teicher, M.D. Ph.D., Martin H. "Wounds That Time Won't Heal: The Neurobiology of Child Abuse." *Cerebrum Dana Foundation*, 1 Oct. 2000, www.dana.org/article/wounds-that-time-wont-heal. *The Mayo Clinic* defines dissociative disorders in being associated with mental disorders that involve experiencing a disconnection and lack of continuity between thoughts, memories, surroundings, actions and identity. "Dissociative Disorders - Symptoms and Causes." *Mayo Clinic*, 17 Nov. 2017, www.mayoclinic.org/diseases-conditions/dissociative-disorders/symptoms-causes/syc-20355215.
[64] Dana Foundation. "Wounds That Time Won't Heal: The Neurobiology of Child…" *Dana Foundation*, 1 Oct. 2000, www.dana.org/article/wounds-that-time-wont-heal.

You are struggling with the effects of what happened to you, but you are pushed to go to college and excel like everyone else. However, emotionally, you have not evolved past that seven-year-old child.

Though your body grew to a young adult, your emotional and social skills have not caught up. For instance, you may engage in a relationship at 21, but your 7-year-old self, desires to be protected. If the mate can't fulfill those needs, they are ousted. You move on to the next. The behavior becomes a never-ending cycle of nothingness, chasing love and fulfillment all because of the 7-year-old that needs to be whole.

In order to interrupt this lack of development, we must engage in consistent and intentional action that pushes us in the realm of growth. But first, it is important to recognize the issue at hand and get to the root of what caused it. This is a process, and the undoing of what has been done, this takes time, oft times the professional help of a psychologist or psychotherapist and patience. It is important to conduct a self-inventory of who you are and who you hope to become.

Next, you'll want to identify your deficits and strengths, and finally map a strategy to start moving your life in the direction you desire it to go in. You want to work that last step like your life and every future generation of your family lives are dependent on it. Because it does.

> Do you often feel stuck in your life? If so, explain how. Then, pick someone you can trust and tell. Seek professional assistance. I have a source on my site as well.

_____

_____

_____

_____

_____

Molestation marks us in different ways. I know these topics are intense, and I thank you for hanging in there with me. More importantly, I thank you for being willing to begin to look at yourself differently and recognize that some of your lifelong struggles are not your fault. I don't aim to shift the blame, but truthfully, you've endured something that no man, woman, or child should ever have to experience, and it's impacted you. It's shaped who you are. But you can change. You can move beyond what happened to you. You can heal.

Please, please, keep reading.

Section Three

THE STRATEGY

In a live television interview on the Trinity Broadcast Network, Thomas Dexter Jakes said, "Some people refuse to get well...because they have built a system around dysfunction." This reminded me of something God told me personally, that I believe will be instrumental for you as well.

As we've explored in the previous sections of this book, the aftermath of childhood sexual abuse can be crippling in a number of ways. It is completely possible for a survivor to live a seemingly "normal" life, one that exhibits no sign of being confused by their identity, suffering from low self-esteem or the spirit of isolation, or caught in an abusive relationship. These marks of molestation can create a system of dysfunction that appear and feel normal. Unaware of how to heal and to create a life absent of trauma, it becomes easier for a victim to live a life like this, a life of perpetual pain, than to move past what has happened to them. Behavior, relationships, silence, feelings of fear, are components of a system that can insulate a survivor from the healing they deserve, and deep down, really want, but have no idea how to achieve. Healing from the pain of childhood sexual abuse is not something that happens on its own. Ignoring it does not make it disappear. Neither will drugs, alcohol, other relationships or sex. Dismantling the system of dysfunction is intentional work. It is daily work, for a time. It is mental, emotional, and spiritual work. And it is work that cannot be ignored.

Imagine you are walking around in life with a hidden bomb inside of your chest pocket, waiting to explode. As a survivor, that bomb is your pain. Right now, you are carrying all of the hurt, trauma, and bottle- up emotions around inside. All it takes is one trigger—a memory, a person who touches you in the wrong way, someone who innocently says the wrong thing to you, and you will explode.

I know you've heard the phrase, "You can run, but you cannot hide." Those words are so true when it comes to experiences that have hurt us. We can do everything we can to pretend the pain isn't there. We can try to ignore it, distract ourselves, even lie and rewrite our stories as if it never happened. But your emotions don't lie. Your body doesn't lie, and neither does your mind. If your pain is not dealt with, it will continue to fester and build until you just can't hold it anymore. You cannot hide from the truth.

I get it, most people don't deal with the aftermath of molestation. It is so complex. It's hard and painful to face. But running from that pain could cost you so much. The person you are truly meant to be and the life you are meant to live is hidden behind the truth you are trying so hard to run from. Will you allow fear to keep you from your God-given purpose?

In the first section of this book, we looked at successful people who were victims of childhood sexual abuse. Many of them have reached the pinnacle of their industries, and impacted people all over the world with their greatness. Now, we don't know how messy their lives have been behind the scenes. They are people too, which means that, likely, the same feelings of confusion, hurt, anger, resentment, and fear have gripped them too. We don't know where they are in their healing process right now, or what it took to get there. But my point is this—if they survived, so can you. If they could find their footing and identity in this world, so can you. If they can succeed, in spite of what happened to them, so can you.

Imagine what could be possible for your life if you were able to face what happened to you and arrive at a place of acceptance and healing. Imagine yourself flourishing fully into who you were meant to be. For you, that may be a successful career.

It could be writing a book or producing movies. Maybe it's ministry, mentoring youth, motherhood, fatherhood, or a healthy marriage. Maybe it's finally starting that non-profit. It is whatever greatness is for *you*. This is not about fame—it's about freedom.

You can still fulfill your purpose in this life. In fact, it is why you survived your abuse. Healing will open up the door for you to step into your full self, your greatest self, and have the life you are meant to live. Your abuse put you in a shell. It made you self-conscious, shy, and insecure. But that it not who you are. Your abuse is not who you are. You are not broken or unworthy. You are a strong person. You are a capable person. You are a person who was born for a purpose. You were born to be seen, heard, and to take up space in this world. You are not here to be hidden.

My hope is that you will begin to work through your experiences so you will not be forever handcuffed to the hurt you've experienced. It's time to reclaim your life. It's time to live.

In this section, we'll look at some practical strategies for how to begin to heal from molestation. As you begin your journey, you will find your own way. This book is here to guide you to as you begin to explore your personal path to healing past pain, unearthing the emotions that you've buried, and growing through what happened to you all those years ago.

I have to be honest, when you are committed to it, healing will be complicated. You may never truly "get over your abuse." For most of us, there is no such thing. But you can live and thrive in spite of it. You can resent less and love more. You can take the power of out your fear, your hurt, and your pain. Trust me, you can. I'm doing it.

This book is about personal healing. So, while I am an advocate of getting support during this process, there will be parts of this journey that you will have to travel alone. Not in the sense of being completely abandoned by other people, but often we are left to sort through our own feelings and find our own path to resolving inner conflict. No one can, or should, tell you how you feel. Abuse affects us all in different ways. Getting to healing will be different for all of us too. Seek support when you need it but be comfortable in solitude at times too. Being alone is healthy when you know it's what you need to do, as opposed to being forced there out of fear. The important part is knowing the difference.

Who Will Help You Heal?

Start with the Person in the Mirror

With all of that said, I cannot stress this enough—you cannot completely heal alone. The spirits of isolation and control desire to keep you away from healing, healthy spaces, and from developing a fulfilling community of people that can push your growth. You need support, some person or people who can remind you that you are not what happened to you. Someone to reflect your wholeness back to you. Someone who can affirm you. Someone who can help you to wash away all of the lies that have covered you since you were molested, and help you to write a new story, a true story, about who you really are.

You may be hesitant to open up to someone right now. Even finding the right mental health professional or pastor or spiritual leader who can trust can take time. So, until you can find the person or people to support you in your healing process, you can start with affirmations.

By saying positive things to yourself every day, you will begin to feel yourself change. Affirmations help to heal you from the inside out and are a tool to help rewire your mind to start eliminating what is untrue and replace those negative beliefs with what is actually true about yourself and your life. It might take some time to believe them, but keep at it.

Here are some things to repeat to yourself every day. Look at yourself in the mirror, and tell yourself these words:

- I didn't deserve it.
- I am special, and because of that specialness the enemy hoped to silence me and dim my light. My light may flicker, but it's not burned out.
- It shouldn't have happened! However, it did, and I am the stronger because of it. (Say it until you find that strength).
- I value me.

- I am POWERFUL!

- I am AMAZING!

- I am a CHAMPION!

- I am a WARRIOR!

- I am are a SURVIVOR!

- I am UNSTOPPABLE!

- I can become whatever I want to be! (Make a list of those things you've only dreamed about and desire to one day accomplish. Display them where you can see them daily.)

> Repeat these words, and you will begin
> to feel and finally believe them. Your
> words have power. Use them as tools to
> empower yourself, release your pain,
> and feel stronger every day.

No More Blame

As childhood sexual abuse survivors, it is natural to want to blame someone for what you experienced. You were supposed to be protected, and somehow, there was a time when that didn't happen. There were people who should have been there to fend for you until you could fend for yourself. Let's be honest, you believe those people should have been your parents. But here is the truth.

Parents are the guards of your life, not the god of your life. There are some things that parents cannot prevent. The God of our lives has an omniscient presence that is all seeing. He is always there, and can be everywhere we are, all of the time. Guards, on the other hand, aim to protect, but there are some things that slip by them. At some point in our lives, we were out of our parent's sight. But God was still there.

I know you may be thinking, why would God see what happened to you, and do nothing to stop it? If God is your ultimate protector, why would He allow you to be molested, knowing how it would hurt you so deeply?

When I am searching for that answer, I'm reminded of the story of Job in the Bible. It's the opening chapter of that book that intrigues me most.

There, we find the Satan in conversation with God. God has asked Satan what he was doing, and Satan gives details about how he was roaming around on the earth. God knew that he was looking for someone to afflict, so God offered and even recommended Job. God knew Job's track record of being an upright man, a man who was serious about his relationship with God and honoring and reverencing him, so much so that he saw to it that his family remained pure to ensure God was pleased. Once God offered Job as Satan's next target, Satan went on to say that Job would curse God once his family and possessions were impacted. However, God was convinced of Job's faithfulness, and he told Satan to move forward, but only on the condition that he wouldn't kill Job. In all, God trusted Job, and knew his faith would not falter, regardless of how much pain Satan inflicted upon him.

Growing up, I heard the story of the Job's intense affliction: how his friends blamed him, how he lost his family and property. However, no one mentioned that all of Job's pain was allowed, and even recommended by God because Job could be trusted! Whether you are a Christian or not, I want you to realize that some of the pain you've experienced and survived could very well be because God trusted you to endure it. After being molested, there are countless others who have lost their minds, lost their way, and lost their purpose. But you didn't. You were bruised, but not broken. You may be wandering in some areas of your life, but you are not lost.

A significant part of your healing process is releasing resentment and blame. Once we understand the purpose of our pain, we can forgive our parents and other people who should have protected and guarded us for not being what we expected them to be, and for not doing what we expected them to do.

All this to say, there still might be some hard conversations you need to have, simply to release. But know regardless of who was or was not there for you as a child and in this experience, God was there.

God is still here. He is the only one who can give you the true answers you may need. Ask Him.

Moving Forward

Molestation, whether physical or emotional, has a resounding impact on our forward movement. Some of us have moved forward in some aspect but have remained stagnant in other areas of our lives.

The interception of molestation disturbs the core identity and purpose of a person but seeks to change the trajectory and path that was originally designed for each individual. While the perpetrators, sometimes, don't knowingly seek to impact the future of their victims, their actions, nonetheless, will. The thrill of the feel-good sensation on their genitals and the power of control is a temporary feeling. But the lasting impact of their actions on their victims is life altering.

You were a victim, and you were preyed upon. The perpetrator identified a person who they, for whatever reason, believed was safe enough to pounce on, and weak enough that they would allow them to get away with it.

Like you, this was a hard reality for me to swallow. I asked myself repeatedly, *Why me? Did I do something? Was I the only option or "best" option? Why?* Why us? We can stay stuck in the space of questioning for a lifetime.

However, in order to get unstuck it is important to settle in your mind that while what happened to you may not be what you would have chosen, God allowed it. And when we finally accept what God allows, we have the ability to heal in a way that is deep and real.

When we accept this, we can move forward in a way where we don't settle with broken pieces, but we pick up those pieces in search of becoming whole again. We are worth more than what the person who molested us tried to leave us with.

Our families are worth more. Our purpose is worth more. YOU are worth more! There's more to you than this!

There is more beyond the façade of the hard exterior that you have masqueraded with all your life. This next level will take a level of vulnerability that you haven't probably already experienced before. This new level of openness won't be comfortable at first, but the more you practice it in safe places, God will grant you the necessary tools that will allow you to press past the discomfort of it.

You can move forward. Start walking toward your freedom.

Ditch the Default

Moving and growing from that arrested place is not a cake walk. However, the first step in the direction of freedom is the courage to change your heart towards what's always been. Let me explain.

Nearly 4 years ago, on October 2, 2016, God gave me this revelation as I sat on the side of my bed. I believe it was not only applicable to me but to you as well as we deal with the issue of molestation. This is what I recorded from that time:

> *You are laying in LoDebar[65] and you must ditch the default. There have been life situations that happened early on that tried to take hold of who you are and how you would be. These situations dictated your personality, your level of relationship, your perspective on who you are and what you have on the inside of you. But, just like a computer system, you have a choice in accepting the default or doing a total wipe. Daily, you have been simply restarting your day, but not fully wiping out the entire system.*

---

[65] Mephibosheth was the grandson of King Saul. As a kid he was dropped by a nurse and was crippled for life in 2 Samuel 4:4. He became an outcast and left to live in a town called LoDebar. LoDebar was a place that meant no pasture-or not fruitfulness, or production. However, King David called him from that LoDebar to bless his life.

Those words changed me forever. As I mediated on each part of what God said to me that day, I realized that not only did I need to accept what happened to me, but I needed to go deeper with my healing. I couldn't stay on the surface, where it was safe. Getting up every day and going about my life wasn't enough. Accepting my life as is, telling myself, "This is just how I am," wasn't enough, because it was lie. I had become a shell of myself as a result of my abuse.

That was my default. But it was time for me to truly live beyond my abuse. I needed to wipe my entire system.

It is easier to remain the same than to make a change. Autopilot and relying on our default level require less effort, and it can be enough to get through your day and survive. Whether it's your favorite route that you take to work every day or your favorite recipe to whip up at home, the regularity of a task becomes an ingratiated action and usually comes without much thought. The system of dysfunction that you have been living in is exactly the same. You are so used to going through the motions and repeating the same patterns, cycles, and behaviors that to do anything else feels impossible. But I am here to tell you that it is far from impossible. You are equipped to change. You can change. You can create a new default for yourself, your relationships, and your life.

Your default is the person you were created to be, and the purpose you were meant to live out. Your default is freedom. Your default is true happiness.

Finding your **H.A.A.P.I** place is your new default. Your H.A.A.P.I place is your path to joy beyond your abuse.

To free yourself from the bondage of abuse, you must incorporate these things into your life:

- ❖ Humility
- ❖ Acknowledgement
- ❖ Accountability
- ❖ Practice
- ❖ Intentionality

These are a set of strategies that have and are guiding my healing, my walk to freedom, and I know they can do the same for you.

HUMILITY

Humility may be the hardest strategy of all of these, but it is the most necessary. Humility is hard because it requires a lowliness, and to look at ourselves as we look at others. Humility grows character, the type of character required to move forward and to be free.

Because of our molestation, most of us have developed an exterior that is hard for love to penetrate. We've also developed a need to control and dominate. Because we were taken advantage of, we have determined in our minds that we will never be put in a situation again in which we are at the mercy of someone else.

In a sense, we become the perpetrator. However, when we soften our hearts towards what happened to us, we posture our spirits to receive the necessary assistance, whether spiritually or naturally, to move beyond the place of stagnancy to maturity.

- Humility requires honesty. Honesty is necessary to understand the reality of the act of molestation that you faced years ago, and that its far-reaching impact still holds you in bondage in some ways. To be honest, we have to cast aside pride. Pride is sometimes is a part of the residue that comes from the impact of molestation, and it is also the biggest blocker of humility. Here are some everyday instances of what pride can look like. Remember, pride makes no announcements, it is often very subtle. For instance:Instead of asking for help with a task, you insist on always doing it alone.

- When offered something personal that you need, you refuse it.

- When someone texts you or sends you a message, you take forever to respond. The person on the other end is awaiting your response, and that feeling alone puts you in control. You won't admit it, but you subconsciously enjoy this. You like to make them wait. (Crazy,right?)

- You have a hard time saying thank you and meaning it! Prideful folks are the most ungrateful people around. Prideful people carry with them an heir of entitlement.

  If they do ever say "thank you," it's generic and often insincere. It is often reflected in similar language like: "Thanks for EVERYTHING!" Specificity makes them feels too vulnerable and open. So, because of the pride, they won't be caught appearing "ungrateful" AND also because of the pride, they dare not specifically tell you what they are appreciative of. It corners them to much. Their being too specific about what they are grateful for reveals too much of their need and makes them feel vulnerable.

- Prideful folks are insanely selfish. So much so that their display of love and appreciation, if ever, is private instead of public. Their every move is calculated (concerned with what others think if they do this or that), so their display of love is often never public and open. You know somebody that fits this category. They're the ones that love to hit you in the DMs instead of posting on your wall.☺

I think you get the picture, being full of pride is the opposite of humility. I could go on forever, because I use to live here. It was a part of a place of comfort. But I had to intercept the madness.

Be real, what are some areas you are your life where you have seen pride rear its ugly head? Write them out in the section below:

_____

_____

_____

_____

_____

_____

_____

_____

_____

_____

_____

_____

ACKNOWLEDGMENT

Acknowledgement is a foundational concept to grasp as you move forward in the healing process. Once we really get to the core of an issue and understand the foundations on which our actions have been built, we then have the awareness to move forward in building strong relationships with ourselves and then with others.

Acknowledgement, by definition, means "to admit to be real or true, to recognize the existence of. To recognize the authority, validity or claim of, to indicate or make known the receipt of..." Acknowledgement, for the abused, is to is face and speak the truth. And that starts with these simple words: *I WAS MOLESTED.*

You may have seen this book's title or a video about the book, and cringed. We know it happened, but nobody else does. In fact, some many of us won't even call it that.

We can even form our lips and say "MOLEST, MOLESTED, MOLESTATION." If we do say those words, there are others of us that won't associate ourselves or our experience with it. We don't want to acknowledge or accept what happened. But it did. We have to acknowledge it.

Acknowledgment looks like:

- ❖ Admitting what happened to you and saying it out loud.
- ❖ Admitting that you were hurt and traumatized by what happened.
- ❖ Recognizing how molestation has impacted your life.
- ❖ Talking about the details of some of your molestation experiences with those that you trust.

Let's practice some acknowledging:

Step 1:

Say it with me:

I WAS MOLESTED AND I WASN'T MY FAULT!

I WAS MOLESTED BUT IT'S NOT WHO I AM!

Step 2:

Say this:

MY MOLESTATION HURT ME.

IT WAS PAINFUL.

IT WAS DISAPPOINTING.

THAT PERSON (NAME THEM) BETRAYED MY TRUST.

THAT PERSON (NAME THEM) STOLE MY INNOCENCE FROM ME.

THAT PERSON (NAME THEM) NO LONGER HAS CONTROL OVER ME.

Step 3:

Think about how you believe molestation has had an impact in your own life, and list those areas out in the section below:

_____

_____

_____

_____

_____

_____

_____

_____

_____

_____

_____

_____

ACCOUNTABILITY

Let's look at what accountability really means: "To subject to the obligation to report, explain, or justify something; responsible, answerable, is the definition of what it means to be accountable. To be obligated to someone, to report and explainable, to answer to someone..."

Accountability, especially for adults can be difficult. To think about allowing ourselves to be vulnerable to another person, to explain ourselves in any way, immediately makes us tense and resistant. When it comes to being accountable around our molestation experiences, we are talking about sharing our most secret thoughts and struggles, as opposed to keeping them bottled up and to ourselves.

To involve another in our personal growth is actually 'anti-adult' by the standards we've set. We've been groomed to do life alone.

But to consciously assign someone you trust and respect to police the intimate details of your life is admirable and honorable. It does not make you less of an adult, or weak. Allowing others in is actually one of the strongest things you will ever do. With accountability, you publicly sign up for change. You take a courageous step forward in the process of healing. You openly commit to being better.

List a few people right now who you trust and respect, and who are worthy enough for you to share your struggle with. Come up with a plan for you to move forward and connect with them on a level that real and true.

<u>Map that out in the section below:</u>

How will you communicate? Via written letter, email, text or phone? Facetime? How often will you check in with them? These people can be professionals or tried and true trusted companions and friends.

_____

_____

_____

_____

_____

_____

_____

_____

_____

_____

_____

_____

PRACTICE

True change comes through consistency. True change comes through doing.

As I was putting the final elements of this manuscript, I was reminded of a biblical text about Luke Chapter 17 verses 11-14. In this chapter, there we TEN men who suffered from a skin disease. When they heard that Jesus would be near a village in Samaria and Galilee, they stood at the village gate waiting and begging for Jesus to help them. He noticed them and immediately gave them instructions. Verse 14 states, "When He saw them, He told them, "Go and show yourselves to the priests." It goes further, "And while they were going, they were healed." Many times, when we've experienced intense pain, we want to sulk and settle in a space of stagnancy. No telling how long those ten men were at the gate and suffered. As soon as Jesus saw them, he told them to **MOVE!**

And as they moved, or went forward, their healing became more and more evident. These men practiced their freedom from the disease. And we must practice by doing as well.

Everything in this book was shared with the purpose of helping you to see that you were not alone in this. You were not the only one that was violated. We've all struggled, and we've all survived. Your survival lets me know that you have the ability to be greater than you already are. Now that you've been reminded of that, I want you to do yourself, and the world, the honor of committing to conquer. To change. To put everything, you've read and learned here into practice. This book was not written to entertain you, it was written to empower you. It's time to practice greatness in your own life.

Just like learning to dance, mastering a new instrument, learning to code computers, or any other skill, healing takes practice.

It is a commitment to consistency, even when it's hard, emotionally exhausting, and uncomfortable. It's been said that "practice makes perfect." But in this case, you are not practicing for perfection. You are practicing for progress, for power, and for the purpose of growing and changing to better yourself for you and for the people around you. Though it can be fearful, you must press past this fear.

In combatting fear, you have to make a decision. Will you allow fear to keep you from what you want? Will you allow it to keep you in bondage? Voiceless? Unable to choose—happiness, love, acceptance? Will you allow fear to submerge, to drown you, to keep you locked down and locked away forever?

Or do you want to learn to swim? Not just in the kiddie pool or three feet of water. I mean swim in the deepest, most calming, most beautiful waters possible.

Where you can stretch your muscles and push yourself beyond what is comfortable and easy and into what is possible. That is what life is like when you choose freedom over deep-seated fear. Fear is crippling, but it's time to **MOVE!**

If you want to live past the experiences that threated to drown you, you have to consciously turn away any thing that requires you to live in fear. A while back, I shared with you that I'd conquered one of my biggest fears and learned to swim in deep waters. With deep level swimming, I was determined to no longer allow the fears I had created of possibly drowning outweigh my desire to enjoy the water. So, I took the necessary steps to ensure I learned the proper techniques to release my fears and hold on to freedom.

You may need a support system, like a therapist or a group, or a church you can trust, to be your guide into the deep waters of your fears, like my swimming instructor was for me. Whatever it takes to get you into the deep end of the pool, find that.

Go back to it again and again. And never forget—you are buoyant—unsinkable.

Practice healing by developing humility to keep growing, acknowledging the impact of your pain, and finding trusted folks to connect with in times of struggle. Put these strategies into action consistently and watch your life change as a result.

What are your primary areas of your life are you struggling in? What are some things you can put in place to assist you overcoming those struggles and moving forward?

_____

_____

_____

_____

_____

_____

_____

_____

_____

_____

_____

_____

_____

_____

_____

Are you committed to practicing humility, acknowledging, and accountability in your life? If so, how?

_____

_____

_____

_____

Write about your journey in tackling commitments? Has this been an area of challenge for you? How can you overcome this?

_____

_____

_____

_____

_____

_____

_____

_____

_____

I would challenge you to get a journal where you can record your day-to-day challenges and struggles and how you hurdled over them. Until you can purchase your journal, you can start the process in the section provided below.

_____

_____

_____

_____

_____

_____

_____

_____

_____

_____

_____

INTENTIONALITY

By now you know I love examining the definitions of words, so we are clear about what they actually mean and how to apply those meanings to our lives.

Intentionality is "the act of forthrightly thinking, acting, and challenging prior ways of being; thinking and acting." Intentionality is the upfront confrontation of who we are, how we are, but it requires purposeful action towards change. Intentionality is the last strategy to use to in the process of getting to your H.A.A.P.I place.

Once again, this is about honesty. Not only about ourselves and our behaviors, but about others around us. There are ways in which we are holding ourselves back, and ways in which we are allowing others to do the same. Both must go. Anything, or anyone, that is impeding your path to healing, freedom, and happiness is stunting your growth.

Be willing to release them. For your own sake, for your generations.

I want you to be honest, and list the habits, behaviors, thoughts, and PEOPLE that have been terrible inhibitors in regard to your growth in the section below:

_____

_____

_____

_____

_____

_____

_____

_____

_____

_____

_____

We don't aim to make excuses for our own behaviors, but how have these things or people blocked your progress?

_____

_____

_____

_____

_____

_____

_____

_____

_____

_____

_____

_____

What are some things you can do daily and intentionally to grow in your area of challenge (s)?

_____

_____

_____

_____

_____

_____

_____

_____

_____

_____

_____

_____

_____

A NOTE FOR PARENTS:

PROTECTING OUR CHILDREN

"95% of sexual abuse is preventable through education and awareness."[66]

We've talked a lot about personal healing in this book and taking personal responsibility not for what happened to us, but for healing past it. We know that God allowed our pain, and that there, somehow, was purpose in it. But that doesn't mean that we should sit back and not do everything we can to ultimately help end the epidemic of molestation by educating generations to come. We can prevent further cycles of abuses in families—and we should. We have an intentional responsibility to protect our children. If we don't protect them, who will?

---

[66] Child Molestation Research and Prevention Institute: The Child Molestation Prevention Plan. (n.d.). Child Molestation Research & Prevention Institute. Retrieved from http://www.childmolestationprevention.org/pages/prevention_plan.html

Here are some tips for protecting the children in your life:

TALK TO THEM

Protecting our children begins in the home. If we increase dialogue in our homes, we can prevent more cases of childhood sexual abuse. We have to talk about it. We have to talk about what has happened to us. We have to talk about the stories of molestation in the news and how women, men, and children have been hurt and impacted by those experiences. Our children need to understand what abuse is. If we hide it, they will hide it too if it happens to them.

I remember first opening up to my children about the complexity of molestation. It was an intense time. I have a son and a daughter, and I spoke with them in the same room, but they had different reactions. I didn't want to project or instill fear, but I did want to uncover how slick and sly this spirit that operates in people could be and it was important to expose them to that truth. It was a tough talk, but a necessary one. Many times, the innocence of a child can turn into naiveté. We owe them more than that.

LEARN TRAITS OF MOLESTORS AND TEACH THEM

- Family and acquaintance child sexual abuse perpetrators have reported that they look for specific characteristics in the children they choose to abuse.

- Perpetrators report that they look for passive, quiet, troubled, lonely children from single parent or broken homes. [67]

- Perpetrators frequently seek out children who are particularly trusting and work proactively to establish a trusting relationship before abusing them.[68]

---

[67] 17 Elliott, M., Browne, K., & Kilcoyne, J. (1995). Child sexual abuse prevention: What offenders tell us. Child Abuse & Neglect, 5, 579-594

[68] De Bellis, M. D., Spratt, E. G., & Hooper, S. R. (2011). Neurodevelopmental biology associated with childhood sexual abuse. Journal of Child Sexual Abuse, 20(5), 548-587.

- Not infrequently, this extends to establishing a trusting relationship with the victim's family as well.[69]

In addition to talking to our children more about what molestation is and its impact, we should also teach them what a perpetrator acts like, so they can be mindful of these types of people who are seeking to hurt them.

There are traits that most abusers, molesters, or perpetrators have in common. Some that are evident to me included being cunningly charismatic, masterfully manipulative, and controlling, performing acts to gain trust, and, when confronted, dismissing/underplaying the concerns of the victim.

I remember wanting to confront my spiritual leadership and seek help after understanding the impact of what happened to me.

---

[69] 17 Elliott, M., Browne, K., & Kilcoyne, J. (1995). Child sexual abuse prevention: What offenders tell us. Child Abuse & Neglect, 5, 579-594.

In my naivety, I was talked out of "telling." Instead, I was coerced by my molester into believing that seeking wisdom and guidance would have a "negative" impact. This manipulation only allowed the perpetrator to gain greater access to my heart and manipulate me with stories about her own abuse and past. Instead of feeling hurt and strong enough to tell someone who could help me, I wound up feeling sympathetic towards her pain. This was artful manipulation at its finest.

LET THEM KNOW THEY CAN TRUST YOU

Your children should always be assured that if they cannot talk to anyone else, they can *always* come to their parents. Resist the urge to judge or place blame when they do, whether it's about something as serious as molestation or small as stealing candy from store. Children need people in their lives who they can trust. Create safe space for conversation.

If you don't, they will be more susceptible to predators throughout their lifetime. They will find refuge in them instead.

WATCH OUT FOR SIGNS OF ABUSE

Because children are often molested by people in authority and who they trust, love, and respect, probing children about the people in their lives and how they are interacting with them is key. If a child is uncomfortable in the presence of an adult, does not want to be touched by that person or spend time with them, that may be indicative of a problem. A small act of abuse can create a cyclical pattern of dysfunction for a family and a community. We have to remain vigilant.

One source said:

> *Often those who have been molested and suffered any abuse turn to unhealthy coping mechanisms that later have a cyclical impact on their families, their communities, and the world at large.*

*Researchers call this the "**Lifetime Burden**"[70] of abuse. The study also reported that CSA alone is accountable for about one per cent of the global burden of disease, but it is likely to be a risk factor for several other conditions like alcohol consumption, illegal drug usage, development of mental disorders, and spread of sexually transmitted diseases, which when pooled, are accountable for over 20% of the global burden.[71]*

If your child suddenly starts drinking, using drugs, or "acting out" emotionally, ask if they are willing to talk to you about what is happening in their lives. Gently probe to find out more and ask about abuse.

Seek help from a therapist, counselor, or professional who specializes in adolescents if your child is resistant to talking to you, or if you need some guidance on how to approach the topic.

---

[70] Dr. Bessel van der Kolk, in essence describes *the Lifetime Burden* theory that researchers suggest happens with victims of abuse. He says, "Is it any wonder, then traumatized individual themselves cannot tolerate remembering it and that they often resort to using drugs, alcohol, or self-mutilation to block out their unbearable knowledge? P. 18.

[71] London, K., Bruck, M., Ceci, S., & Shuman, D. (2003) Disclosure of child sexual abuse: What does the research tell us about the ways that children tell? *Psychology, Public Policy, and Law, 11*(1), 194-226.

CONCLUSION

This is a book I never wanted to write. I avoided it because I didn't think it was necessary. But it is. For me and everyone else who has read or will read these words.

Yes, I owed this book to myself. But more than that, I wanted to give the world an example of what healing can look like. I wanted to provide a real-life journey about what it means to face hard things, to unearth past hurt or unaddressed pain. I knew this before, but I definitely know it now—we can become champions of our past. Once we conquer and face it, we can legitimately aid the world around us. I hope I've done that here.

This healing work is by no means easy. Writing this book was a part of my process, and healing is a journey that I still walk every day. I am not where I used to be, but I am still working to put my pride aside, seek humility, acknowledge my pain, and be accountable to those who I've trusted to support me. I still affirm myself and remind myself often that my abuse does not define me, and that there was nothing I did to deserve it. I journal out my struggles. I am intentional about my work. I am committed to the practice of healing. All of the things and strategies that I shared with you. I do them too, still.

And even with all of the work I've done to move past my abuse, *it still hurts*. So, I don't want you to believe that it won't pain you as you begin to open these wounds. There will be triggers, but they won't have the same power. Thomas Dexter. Jakes articulated it much better than I ever could, "there's pain in recovery."

However, he added, "Just because it hurts doesn't mean it isn't getting any better."

You will get better. You will get stronger. You have to. Do it for you.

I'm rooting for you! We're in the growth journey together! ~Dr. Nes ♥

RESOURCE LIST

Firstly, visit our site at **www.molestedbutinvested.com** for an opportunity to win one-hour of free therapy!

1.   **Rape, Abuse & Incest National Network (RAINN)**-www.rainn.org

2.   National Sexual Assault Hotline--800-656-HOPE

3.   National Sexual Violence Resource Center-https://www.nsvrc.org/statistics
 https://www.nsvrc.org/sites/default/files/2012-03/Publiations_NSVRC_ResourceList_Child-sexual-abuse-prevention.pdf

4.   **Great List**-https://greatist.com/live/sexual-assault-survivor-resources#hotlines-and-call-centers

5.   Child Welfare Information Gateway-https://www.childwelfare.gov/organizations/?CWIGFunctionsaction=rols:main.dspList&rolType=Custom&RS_ID=77

6.   11 Facts about Child Abuse-https://www.dosomething.org/us/facts/11-facts-about-child-abuse#fn2

7.   Public Health-https://www.publichealth.org/resources/sexual-abuse/

Contact Author

Would you like to schedule a book signing or speaking event with the author?

Complete one of the contact forms at

www.iamdrnes.com or www.molestedbutinvested.com

Follow Us

@iamdrnes
@molestedbutinvested

Desire to Write a Book?

Contact our publisher at
www.drnesintl.com

Made in the USA
Columbia, SC
16 April 2022

59083923R00115